"Winn Collier has learned through the twists and turns of his own life the difference between faith and certainty. When life pushes us to the edge between belief and disbelief, some rush back to unquestioning faith and others rush away to unquestioning disbelief. This book helps us learn to stay in the place of tension that is true both to the realities of our experience and to the God who made and loves us."

— DANIEL TAYLOR

author of *The Myth of Certainty* and *In Search of Sacred Places*

"By sharing his journey, Winn has put into words the struggle of engaging in the mysteries of knowing God. His conversational style causes the reader to enjoy the insights gained by his honest search for intimacy with our Creator. I would recommend this book to anyone seeking a thoughtful, heartfelt approach to knowing God."

— KEN EDWARDS, MDiv, MA

counselor

"*Restless Faith* is an invitation to honesty. In a culture where we are constantly tempted to choose cosmetic image over raw truth, it is refreshing to hear someone speak so candidly about the real terrain on the path of faith. With the voice of a fellow traveler, Winn invites us to wrestle with the reality of our lives as we dance with the mystery of God."

— DEBBIE SMITH, MA

executive director, Center for Women in Medicine

restless faith

Holding On to a God Just Out of Reach

WINN COLLIER

NAVPRESS®

BRINGING TRUTH TO LIFE

OUR GUARANTEE TO YOU

We believe so strongly in the message of our books that we are making this quality guarantee to you. If for any reason you are disappointed with the content of this book, return the title page to us with your name and address and we will refund to you the list price of the book. To help us serve you better, please briefly describe why you were disappointed. Mail your refund request to: NavPress, P.O. Box 35002, Colorado Springs, CO 80935.

The Navigators is an international Christian organization. Our mission is to reach, disciple, and equip people to know Christ and to make Him known through successive generations. We envision multitudes of diverse people in the United States and every other nation who have a passionate love for Christ, live a lifestyle of sharing Christ's love, and multiply spiritual laborers among those without Christ.

NavPress is the publishing ministry of The Navigators. NavPress publications help believers learn biblical truth and apply what they learn to their lives and ministries. Our mission is to stimulate spiritual formation among our readers.

ISBN 1-57683-711-4

Cover design by The DesignWorks Group, Charles Brock; www.thedesignworksgroup.com
Cover photo by Photonica
Creative Team: Steve Parolini, Arvid Wallen, Kathy Mosier, Glynese Northam

Some of the anecdotal illustrations in this book are true to life and are included with the permission of the persons involved. All other illustrations are composites of real situations, and any resemblance to people living or dead is coincidental.

Unless otherwise identified, all Scripture quotations in this publication are taken from the HOLY BIBLE: NEW INTERNATIONAL VERSION® (NIV®). Copyright © 1973, 1978, 1984 by International Bible Society. Used by permission of Zondervan Publishing House. All rights reserved. Other versions used include: THE MESSAGE (MSG). Copyright © 1993, 1994, 1995, 1996, 2000, 2001, 2002. Used by permission of NavPress Publishing Group; the *Contemporary English Version* (CEV) © 1995 by American Bible Society. Used by permission; the *New American Standard Bible* (NASB), © The Lockman Foundation 1960, 1962, 1963, 1968, 1971, 1972, 1973, 1975, 1977, 1995; and the *English Standard Version* (ESV), copyright © 2001 by Crossway Bibles, a division of Good News Publishers. Used by permission. All rights reserved.

Collier, Winn, 1971-
  Restless faith : holding on to a God just out of reach / Winn Collier.
    p. cm.
  Includes bibliographical references.
  ISBN 1-57683-711-4
  1. Spirituality. 2. Christian life. 3. Faith. I. Title.
  BV4501.3.C646 2005
  248.4--dc22
                          2005016584
Printed in Canada

1 2 3 4 5 6 / 09 08 07 06 05

dedication

To Miska, my soul mate in the mystery.
You encourage me to dive into the depths,
even when they are dark.
Better yet, you dive in with me.
Much delight is in my life because of you.
I love you with all my heart.

If the book we are reading does not wake us, as with a fist hammering on our skull, why then do we read it? Good God, we would also be happy if we had no books, and such books as make us happy we could, if need be, write ourselves. But what we must have are those books which come upon us like ill-fortune, and distress us deeply, like the death of one we love better than ourselves, like suicide. A book must be an ice-axe to break the sea frozen inside us.

—FRANZ KAFKA

contents

acknowledgments

he mystery of God both drew and frightened her." This is how Mark Salzman described one of his nuns, Sister Helen, in *Lying Awake*. Salzman could have been describing me. In the process of giving myself space to explore God's otherness in these pages, my emotions have kept pace with Sister Helen. I am enticed toward an experience with this God who is distinctly himself, who resists the small-minded descriptions I want to label him with and the shallow, empty corners I continually attempt to push him into. This God is alive, bold, and never boring.

Yet this God who pushes back in his resilient act of defiance is foreboding. I don't know what to do with him. Rather than fitting into my scheme, he arranges it so that I have to yield to his. He makes me squirm. He makes me nervous. Sometimes he makes me frightened.

Because God eludes my tightly clenched grip, I question and struggle. I have doubts. These pages fumble around a good bit with my uncertainties, with my doubts, with the realities of a God who is beyond. Yet doubts can be a way of engagement, a way of staying in the conversation. God, it seems, likes us to keep talking. "Doubts are the ants in the pants of faith," Buechner says. "They keep it awake and moving." My faith, then, is vigorous indeed.

There are many to thank for this book. Lil Copan actually got it started when she encouraged a writer to write. Steve Parolini's enthusiasm for the ideas and the words in these pages made me believe there was actually something here worth saying. Peter Hiett showed me ways that a pastor could engage the God of the Scripture while giving away his own honest story — it gave me hope and was incredibly inviting. Michael Cusick and Ken Edwards have spoken life to me, and trite as it might sound, that says quite a lot. In a few important places, Switchfoot has dared me to move, and I am truly thankful. Downtown Community Fellowship humbles me with their generosity — providing space for my passions and explorations is a true gift. Margaret Feinberg asked how she could help — what a question! This book is the answer. Thank you.

My mom and dad have put up with my questions longer than anyone. Somehow they fought the urge to tell me to stop asking, "Why?" though I'm sure at times it would have made perfect sense to do just that. Thank you for loving me — that is the best gift a son can ever receive. My sister Vonda has always believed in me. Sis, I hope you know I believe in you too.

My boys, Wyatt and Seth, have brought wonder into my world. They have shown me fresh faces of God. Wyatt, I love when you scream at the snowman. Never stop screaming. Seth, your squinty-eyed, wide-mouthed grin tells me there is joy in this world. I take great delight in you.

Miska, no one has loved better, lived more truly, or spoken more words from the Spirit than you. I embrace you, and I know there is a God. And he is very, very good.

WINN COLLIER
Advent 2004

confessions of a pilgrim

Holy *is our best word to describe [this] life — the human aliveness that comes from dealing with God-Alive. We're most human when we deal with God. Any other way of life leaves us less human, less ourselves.*

— EUGENE PETERSON

*C*all it depression, a chemical imbalance, or just an everyday case of exhaustion, but I was in the gutter. For three years of grad school, I had kept an insane pace: taking sixteen hours a semester, driving four hundred miles a week between school and two jobs located in two cities, and trying to maintain some semblance of a healthy relationship with a woman who lived six and a half hours away.

It never occurred to me that, at some point, my body might rebel. And rebel it did. Over a few months, I spiraled into heavy despair. I couldn't eat, and it took all my energy to focus on menial tasks such as slipping on my pants or opening the mail. All I wanted to do was sleep; most days, I dragged myself out of bed and through the rituals of showering and shaving and driving to work just so I could lock the door and collapse on the floor. When lunchtime arrived, I would drive home for an hour to take a nap.

One summer evening, I walked outside with the cordless phone and called a friend who had spoken wise words to me in previous times of chaos. He answered the phone, and my desperate words spilled out. When the flood stopping pouring over the dam, there was silence on the other end.

After a few seconds, he interrupted the awkward quiet and asked, "Winn, are you willing to be wrong?"

The question seemed out of order, as if he had missed the point or hadn't heard the weight of my words. However, his query couldn't have been more skillfully lodged, and those seven simple words probed long-forgotten contours of my heart. I was willing to endure many things: difficulty, discipline, hard work, challenges, and numerous other noble-sounding feats of the will. Yet there was one thing I would never accept: being wrong. My life, my pursuits, and my view of God all held a common assumption: It was my *responsibility* to get it right.

I was a typical firstborn, and I readily embraced the role of the achiever. I was first in my class academically, moderately successful athletically, and a leader in every arena I entered. I possess an entrepreneurial spirit, so I often scoured for the most hopeless situation, marking it as a place where I could gallop in to save the day.

During my freshman year in college, a few buddies and I purposefully joined the most berated and scoffed-at fraternity on campus. We wanted to carve out a piece of history for ourselves, and we were convinced we could dig in and turn this fledgling group around. We did. For most of my life, I had the Midas touch, and successes poured in, seemingly a sure thing. Life was to be conquered. Obstacles were simply where I proved my grit. Given enough time and sweat, there was nothing I couldn't figure out, overcome, or subdue.

Without recognizing it, I had embraced a secular, Westernized worldview in which individual will and acumen are perceived as the primary means to achievement and lack thereof as the only barriers. This abandonment to self-reliance harmonized well with the Enlightenment-influenced vibe in which "the modern knower engages in the knowing process believing that knowledge inevitably leads to progress."[1] With enough sweat and scientifically styled precision, I believed nothing could elude my grasp.

Not surprisingly, this thinking spilled over into my view of God. God was wise and perfect, and it was our task, with a slight verbal nod given to the work of the Spirit, to figure him out. Defining God and his ways properly was the aim, and theological precision was the tool that would allow me to get there.

Though I would never have used such language, what I had always attempted to do with life was exactly what I now intended to do with God: conquer. My foray into graduate theological education was, in reality, one more step toward conquering God. And this, I soon found out, was a dicey proposition.

My first years of studying theology were intoxicating, but the further I delved into my studies, the more tenuous my hold became on these elusive attempts. There was always someone smarter, an idea more developed, or a theoretical nuance resisting my grasp. One question answered would lead to five more yet to be explored. It was as if God refused to be manipulated, and my frustration grew into a crisis. God simply wouldn't cooperate.

As if seamlessly orchestrated, my other pursuits crumbled the same way. My relationship with Miska, the woman I loved and would thankfully later marry, was in shambles. I was unable to determine if she was "the one," and she wouldn't cooperate by acquiescing and morphing into the exact person I had always "known" I was to marry. My leadership abilities, which had always trumped whatever bad cards were dealt me, folded, and the ministry where I served sputtered. My friends, who had always affirmed my gifts and encouraged my dreams, were distant, and I was left alone to sink deeper into self-doubt. The Midas touch had dissipated. God had eluded my grasp. And I was more terrified than I had ever been.

So on this muggy evening in my front yard underneath a vast, starlit Texas sky, I was forced to face my grim reality: I am not God. My attempts toward perfection, toward absolute knowing, toward attempting to control Deity were entirely futile.

It isn't that endeavoring to explore the vastness of God is an ignoble pursuit; it's just that I am blinded by my vanity. I find it difficult to comprehend that knowing God is not simply possessing a vast array of facts about him.

Rather than trusting the good Creator, enjoying his gifts when they are offered, and being content in the mysteries of divine ways, I manipulate with painstaking calculation and intellectual dissection. I seek to control, and I strive to subdue. I am determined to know — not an intimate knowing lovers revel in but a manipulative knowing like that of a frantic scientist ripping apart his latest experiment, reducing the mystery to spare parts and junk metal. What I find, however, is that this God I attempt to conquer is much larger than I could ever imagine, and he doesn't conform to my categories or succumb to my whims.

My obsession with being right and conquering God is a culturally acceptable way to feed my addiction for control and a clumsy mask for my feverish attempt to keep at bay the foreboding possibility that I might not be as well put together as I put on. My friend's well-placed question was more than an invitation to recognize my limitations and accept a nice dose of humility. It was an invitation to step into a deeper reality of God where I would sit under him rather than over him and any attempts to control him would seem as foolish as trying to bottle the Pacific. It was an invitation to mystery.

The word *mystery* can have a nostalgic ring to it—it conjures images of delving into the intrigue of Sherlock Holmes before drifting to sleep or of wondering what the tightly wrapped box with the red plaid bow might have hidden inside. But these are mysteries in our domain, ones we control. They are fairy tales we weave and experiences that fit nicely within our reality.

True mystery, God's mystery, can be hideously terrifying. His mystery asks us to trust when every instinct pulls us in the opposite direction. His mystery demands we loosen our grip when every internal voice screams at us to stay riveted, unmoved. The kind of mystery God offers is one in which we face our fears, our wounds, our deepest doubts, and all the dark corners of our soul that we have spent our life hiding from and ignoring and glossing over. We step into them, and we hope—not demand—that we find God somewhere in the midst.

This mystery feeds our fears because it dismantles the illusion of certainty. Our earliest experiences are of testing the waters, seeing what we can be certain of and what we can't. *Who can I trust to hold me? What can I touch?*

When our son Wyatt turned one year old, he was just beginning to explore his world, testing the boundaries and constructing his reality. Like responsible parents, we did our best to childproof the house, covering the electrical sockets and putting away anything pointed and everything potentially toxic. Yet his mischievous wonderings always found that one thing we couldn't remove or that one cord we had to leave out.

One of his primary fascinations was with the stove. A few unfortunate mishaps helped him grasp the meaning of hot—he learned this is an unpleasant and possibly painful experience. However, his daring nature moved him to venture to the limits. How close could he get to the stove before it hurt? How long could he touch the window of the oven before it became unbearably painful? As Wyatt grows older, he will continue to explore, and then he will set his limits based on what he can be certain of. This is the way it works with kids and stoves — and with dads and dreams.

The older and wiser we get, the more complex the questions become, but at their core, they are the same. *Who can I trust that I know won't let me down? What can I do that I know God will always respond to? How can I be certain to make life work and get out of it what I want?*

This is why stepping into mystery causes me such pause. It shifts the foundation. It requires that I no longer start with all I have tried and tested, all I know. It requires faith — faith to abandon my delusion that with enough savvy and dogged determination, I can acquire what I need and capture what I demand.

Human experience tells us that nothing we most deeply value—friendships, marriage, children—surrenders to the demands for certainty. I am finding that the sturdy sinews of lasting friendship develop only over time and through disappointments, tears, and hopelessly lonely encounters. A marriage that has deep roots and flashes of ecstasy has traveled many winter seasons when passion was a faded memory and the heart lay scorched by hopes run wild. Although my boys are still young, too young to have been disappointed too severely, the day of disappointments is coming, and I will find out if our nurturing and loving and giving made any difference at all. These relationships can yield great joys, but they are not a science. Heartache and confusion accompany each delight.

Would I think the spiritual journey any different? In matters of the heart, there are few sure things. When it comes to God, we can be certain of two: He will always do what is good, and we will sometimes be disappointed. He will always do what is good because he *is* good and true and just. We will at times be disappointed because our perception of goodness and truth and justice is often strikingly dissimilar from his.

This is the shadowland of mystery: to embrace God even when we can't control him. I want to embrace him, all of him — what I see as well as what I will never see, what I hope for as well as what I am disappointed by, what I can envision enough to believe with vigor and what is a dim memory barely offering enough faith to eke out a mumbled prayer.

Perhaps this is why Jonathan Edwards came to define the study of God as "the teaching of living toward God."[2] True theology is never a dry, intellectual exercise; rather, it is the endeavor to be consumed with the reality of the One who is beyond our categories in such a way that we point in his direction. To live toward God is to move, not to arrive. To live toward God is to taste, not to consume.

But living toward God doesn't carry quite the ring of certitude I am looking for. It doesn't promise fail-safe paths or assure comfortable travels. It doesn't protect me from the sorrow or ravages of the world, the misfortunes I strain to avoid.

Eugene Peterson similarly tags this the path of "going to God" where "Christians travel the same ground that everyone walks on, breathe the same air, drink the same water, shop in the same stores, read the same newspapers, are citizens under the same governments, pay the same prices for groceries and gasoline, fear the same dangers, are subject to the same pressures, get the same distresses, are buried in the same ground."[3] There is no shortcut, no way to detour around the deserts or to navigate away from the storms. There is no way other than plodding an uncertain road. It is, as Peterson says, "a long obedience in the same direction."

But I am frightened to set out on such a journey. Journeys ought to have destinations and well-marked trails. I am accustomed to a precise atlas and mapping programs detailing to the tenth of a mile the entire trip. The notion that journeying, pilgrimage with God, might itself be the end, well, that is just entirely implausible not to mention inefficient.

It is a commonly held belief, supported by plenty of anecdotal evidence, that men do not ask for directions. We are content to drive seventy miles out of our way as long as our male ego escapes unscathed. Not me. While I'm not eager to admit to a stranger at the gas station, "Yes, I'm from out of town," and "Yes, I did get turned around and forget which way was south," there is something else I dislike more: I hate to be lost. To set out on an uncertain journey, one in which I don't know the destination, can't say with confidence how I am getting there, and won't even know when I've arrived, sounds like pure insanity to me.

The last eighteen months have been the most difficult stretch of our six years of marriage. For almost five years, things sailed along smoothly for us. We enjoyed emotional intimacy and sexual fireworks.

I am ashamed to admit it now, but it had become a point of pride for me. I felt I had practically conquered the complexity of marriage, and I was sure I would soon be instructing others on the proper steps to enjoying the bliss Miska and I had created. Then things changed. We brought a new life into the world. And elated as we were to have Wyatt, it was a new dynamic. We also moved across the country from the wild West of Denver to the Deep South of upstate South Carolina. I began a new ministry in a new town with little relational support, and Miska dove headlong into the joy and upheaval of motherhood. Soon we began to see that we had grown apart, quietly living out our lives together and yet alone.

In this place, things that had once happened naturally now required a good deal of effort. At the dinner table we were often silent, and attempts at conversation were often strained. Our spiritual connection felt disjointed and sporadic, and our sexual intimacy sputtered. Miska had always had healthy, robust sexual passions, which made me feel desired and pleasured in. I had always felt confident in my place as a man, wooing her and enjoying her. All these realities suffered severe attrition, and in many respects, I didn't know who I was anymore.

As we began to work through this morass, I became aware of fears I had never owned up to, terrors I had never confessed. I was afraid that Miska would eventually grow disinterested in me and that at some point she would move on to someone better, more attractive, more manly. This radically influenced how I interacted with her. There were times when I lay in bed next to my soul mate with whom I have shared joys and sorrows and was terrified to reach out for her. My heart would pound, and my mind would race. Often, I would lie there and do nothing but sheepishly wonder what had happened to my courage.

One night, Miska remarked that I seemed apprehensive with her. She pried into my heart, and as we talked and explored, I was forced to face my fear of rejection, the fear that I would extend an offer that was refused. I was more afraid of being rejected than I was of shutting down my desires, more committed to protecting my heart than I was to pursuing hers.

I have lived much of my life in this way. I am fearful of the possibility that my hopes might be dashed. It has seemed better not to hope and ensure minimal disappointment than to hope and live with wrecked dreams. I am petrified of mystery.

Mystery means we plunge into questions and embrace uncertainty. It insists we hold on to hope, and we hold . . . and we hold . . . and we hold. It is frightening and unsettling, and all our senses tell us we have made a wrong turn and encourage us to sprint back to certainty and safety.

Yet embracing mystery allows us to embrace God, to see more of who he is rather than who we have insisted he be. Mystery allows us to bring all of who we are — our humanness and our weakness — honestly before God because it rips away the veil of perfection and opens the door to embracing our brokenness. It allows us to bare our souls and trust that there is One who hears even when he doesn't answer.

When I eschew mystery, I shut off my hopes and my heart, and I hide much of who I am from God. Over time, I forget these realities, and then slowly I find I have become someone I in truth am not. But I'm safe — at least for the moment.

I am weary of safety, of tirelessly trying to harness God. I am tired of manipulation and denial. I crave to experience God's reality, even if that means I must die to my own. I am disillusioned by the way I have seen my demands refused and my assumptions dismantled, and I am coming to see this painful process as a grace.

I am far less self-assured than I once was, and I hold tightly to far fewer things than I once did. I might actually be able to listen now, and I might find that God has much to say, even if the words are quieter and never arrive on demand.

In recent days, many guides have aided me along my journey into mystery. Moments of encounter, meaningful experiences, conversations in unexpected times, and a quiet listening to a number of spiritual voices have offered encouragement. Insightful wisdom and kind rebuke, each a grace, have been offered me.

In addition to these, a particular ancient guide has offered his own dose of help and good judgment. This guide is a prophet we know little of other than a short message he spoke to a people living in tattered times. Some were drunk on arrogance, beguiled into believing they had God figured out. Some were struggling to hope, disillusioned by a God whose actions were more peculiar and unsettling than they had ever imagined. This prophet Malachi saw the confusion and the despair, the haughtiness and the belligerent pride. He had words from God, words of hope and life as well as fury and strength. Malachi had heard from God, and he knew that this is what the people — all of them — needed as well. He was a messenger in the right place at the wrong time, and he was tapped to deliver a tome that was astringent and strangely inviting all at once.

Malachi has encouraged me to explore more of God — less of what I have demanded, less of what I have assumed, but always more of God.

In its own way, each of these guides has aided me much in grappling with mystery, but there is much, much more grappling to do. I suspect that if we follow the cues and listen to the voices, we might find our own fears unveiled, and we might find our well-manicured categories imploding. But we will also find God, rich in mercy, who offers us the gift of refusing to be as small as we have made him.

CHAPTER 1

savage grace

Our salute to you tumbles out:
    Lord, sovereign, governor, king
        political images of us before you, gender specific,
        marked by macho.
    Sometimes we speak the terms glibly, out of habit.
    Sometimes we speak them with gravity, counting
    on you.
But sometimes we are brought up short to see,
        yet again,
    that you are not kidding: you are other than us.
    you will not be mocked.

          —WALTER BRUEGGEMANN

"Was not Esau Jacob's brother?" the LORD says. "Yet I have loved Jacob, but Esau I have hated, and I have turned his mountains into a wasteland and left his inheritance to the desert jackals."

          —MALACHI 1:2-3

Sometimes love takes on unlikely shapes and gives off strange aromas. It can surprise you and grab you in places you would never have expected. At times, love can be downright cruel.

I recall childhood memories: disobeying my mom, tormenting my sister, or arguing about coming in after dark. I remember my dad sending me off on a somber trip to my room that in these instances he referred to as "the woodshed." I'm in my thirties, but I still wince when I remember his words, "I love you, son, and this is going to hurt me more than it hurts you." I was always willing to test the assumption, but he never seemed game.

To my eight-year-old mind, *love* just didn't seem to fit the context. Love was an ice-cream cone when the truck with the music rounded our block. Love was a trip to the zoo or playing catch at dusk. Love most certainly had nothing to do with woodsheds.

A commonly accepted reality about God is that he is a God of love. He is kind and compassionate. He oozes with goodness. The stories of God's unparalleled generosity abound. When God's people were desperate for food, the skies opened up, and cakes fell from the clouds. When the people were thirsty, water gushed from a rock. When Jesus walked on the earth, divine compassion was realized: Leprous dads returned home, lame children united with their playmates, and blind paupers abandoned the shame of their street-side begging.

I like this God. He is nurturing, approachable. He is safe. My comfort level dips a bit, however, if I veer from this well-worn path. Somehow, my amicable God doesn't seem quite so good-natured.

God chucked Adam and Eve out of a garden. *For eating a piece of fruit.* Entire city-nations were massacred at God's bidding. Women were not spared. Children received no mercy.[1] In the case of the Amalekites, an entire people was expunged from the historic record. *For doing what nations have always done — expanding their territory, defending their national pride*. Ananias and Sapphira dropped dead after giving to the church a large percentage from the sale of a piece of property. *For a fib — fudging when they told how much of their profit they had given.*[2]

Like Lewis's foursome in *The Lion, the Witch and the Wardrobe* who hear of the "mysterious horror" of Aslan,[3] we knock up against the brutish reality that there is a well-entrenched distinction between God as good (loving, caring, faithful, fatherly) and God as safe (predictable, easy, cozy). Goodness is inherent in God's core essence. Good is one way of describing what he is. Safe, however, is something God has never promised. His is a dangerous goodness.

What kind of God is this? One who abounds in mercy yet also ravages and destroys. A God who is not safe.

One place where these conflicting realities are particularly unsettling is in the message of the prophet Malachi. This dualism is the launching point for his oracle. Malachi begins with a declaration of God's extravagant love for his people, and when the skeptical Israelites ask for testimony to back up his claims, he points to their own ethnic history, the story of Esau and Jacob. Both were Isaac's sons, gifts from God, yet God hated Esau while loving their ancestor Jacob.[4]

This might have been good news for the Israelites, affirming their distaste for their bitter enemy, Esau's Edomite descendants. But I suspect it should be unsettling for many of the rest of us. God was not reacting to some sibling spat or simply remarking on his harsh dislike for a solitary character in biblical history. God decreed — and Malachi affirmed — his utter dispossession of an entire race, the Edomites. Should this make me nervous? I own no lineage to Jacob.

To complicate further, Malachi expounds on the degree of God's utter disdain for Esau's offspring. The viciousness of the words digs deep: "Yet I have loved Jacob, but Esau I have hated, and I have turned his mountains into a wasteland and left his inheritance to the desert jackals."[5]

Wasteland? Desert jackals?

Remember, these ferocious words are given as proof of his *love*. Kind of upsets the categories and sets a fellow on edge. But it also moves me to gingerly explore this paradoxical prophet.

As the Hebrew Bible winds to a close, we find this odd little book, Malachi. It is passed over for multiple reasons: It is short (only fifty-five verses), it is the last witness of an overlooked and misnamed portion of Scripture (the so-called Minor Prophets), and it is the final revelation of the Hebrew Bible. So by the time we get to Malachi, we are tired of drought and pestilence and endless genealogies and are gunning for the excitement of the Gospels and Jesus and those Pharisees who are always scheming themselves into a theological corner.

Yet Malachi is a hinge. On it swings the Old Covenant and the New. On it, the Old Order before Christ closes, and the New Order under Christ opens. Before we escape the tumultuous rampage of God across the previous pages, we are forced to deal with the unsettling paradox of a God who ravages with grace.

We know little of the prophet Malachi. He appeared on the scene, a man destined to deliver a message, and then he disappeared. Both God's insatiable covenant love for his people and his extravagant mercy for those outside the covenant have been building to a climax. The prophetic messages from Yahweh to Israel erupted in Hosea with the scandalous tale of a preacher and a harlot. God's message was as stunning as it was clear: I love you, my whoring people, and no false lover's bed is beyond my reach.

Weaving through Jonah, we find God moving storms and prophets and large fish to extend his gregarious offer of free grace to a people who had done nothing but spit on him, wrinkling their noses in disgust at his message and his people.

And now we bump against Malachi, the final message of God to his chosen people.

The situation to which Malachi spoke was unique. Most prophetic books, especially the minors, were cast in dire times: Micah's message was delivered while Assyria lurked on Israel's borders, destruction imminent. Habakkuk spoke amidst the turmoil of Assyria's fall but in light of the rising storm: the Babylonians crouching to descend while Judah quivered in fear. The prophets primarily wrote to a people on the brink of disaster, suffering exile in Babylonia or facing starvation and ruin.

Not Malachi. Malachi was a postexilic prophet (approximately 530–430 BC). Most who wished to return to their homeland had. Under Zerubbabel, the temple had been rebuilt, and with Nehemiah's keen leadership, the city walls had been restored. Though the Israelites were still under the reign of a foreign power, the Persians proved to be a much kinder sovereign. The Persian kingdom was wealthy, powerful, and cultured, and the Israelites were granted full access to it.[6]

However, if you listened to the people's complaints, you probably wouldn't have picked up on their improved situation. Discontent and demanding, the people brooded. Even worse, they dismissed God as irrelevant to their daily affairs. Void of a crisis or threat of conquest, dulled by relative ease, and embracing the cynicism of their unfulfilled expectations, the people nudged God from his center place.

God became something they used — handy, even helpful, but

something they would pick up when needed and set down when something else grabbed their fancy. In a pinch, God was useful to have around, but as part of everyday existence, he was an afterthought.

Remarkable. The very people of God were treating him like a light switch. Had they forgotten that their history was replete with magnificent tales of grand God-triumphs on their behalf—splitting the seas, plaguing enemies with locusts and boils and frogs, and even on one occasion causing the sun to stand still? God had cared for them, watched over them, delivered them, and fed them. Now they discarded him like an old T-shirt.

Still, God's message to his wayward people began as one might expect: with a firm affirmation of affection and desire. The first words from God are familiar: "I have loved you." There is nothing new here. God has said the same thing since Genesis.

I love you. It's beautiful, and it's simple. It's a phrase that should regularly roll off our tongues and frequently pour into our ears. But instead, it dissolves with time, a bit of its sweetness sucked away with each taste.

God declared utter fidelity, love true and rapturous. He desired them. Yet they were disinterested, sullen, and unmoved. They were bored lovers.

The people's response was lethargic: "Yeah, well, that's nice, but what have you done for us *lately*?"[7] Surely their memory of God's protection, provision, and miraculous intervention hadn't *completely* faded. Or maybe it had. Once boredom slips in, the eyes begin to roam, and whatever is left of passion drifts. It's the way of lost love.

It is akin to my planning a romantic Valentine's Day rendezvous with my wife. After arranging for an all-night babysitter, making dinner reservations, and securing a room at the chic downtown hotel, I take an old-fashioned quill and parchment paper and create an original work of poetry as her invitation to this night of intimacy and amour. The poetic verse is shaky, and the delivery of the invitation is a bit melodramatic. But that's due to nerves. I'm giddy. It's embarrassing. But I'm in love. Miska opens the invitation, reads it reflectively, and then offers a measured response: "I'm appreciative of your kind offer. However, I don't want to commit to this plan quite yet. I'm waiting to see what other offers I get for Valentine's Day this year."

God's people were weighing their options, considering all their possibilities. It wasn't that God was totally out of the picture; it's just that he wasn't the front-runner anymore. They were bored, and they wanted to see what kind of action they might find elsewhere. How had God shrunk so small in their minds?

Malachi decries how they had even brought defiled food to the altar of God. They wanted the routine of a relationship with God, but they didn't want it to require anything from them. So they brought their scraps to temple worship. They had grown so indifferent that they committed the most scandalous insult: They kept up the façade of love while reeking of strange perfume. They wanted to sleep with another lover but still keep their slippers at home in the closet and their toothbrush near the sink. *How* had God shrunk so small in their minds?

One of my favorite places to visit is the South Carolina Botanical Gardens. It's only a few minutes from my house, but stepping into its shaded haven, I feel as if I'm entering another dimension. I love to write there, surrounded by oaks, a pond with its own little tribe of ducks, a perfect little picnic table resting on pine needles, and a full hosta garden. The weather recently has offered the first hint of autumn, and I have grabbed every opportunity to enjoy its hospitable invitation.

Last week, we took Wyatt to the gardens. It was the first time he didn't have to be pushed in a stroller. From his first few steps in, he was entranced. He wanted to walk toward the pond, but he grabbed my hand so I would go with him. It was an uneven path with roots protruding from the towering trees, and he took slight steps, eager but unsure. We got to the pond, and we just stood . . . and stood . . . and stood . . . and stood a little more. I coaxed him back up toward his mom and the picnic tables.

He wanted to stop at every opportunity: to look at the fallen acorns, to touch the leaves, to turn back toward the pond and stare. He insisted we pause again, just to look. I couldn't quite tell what had him so transfixed. There was nothing spectacular as far as I could see. He just wanted to stand and take it all in.

Wyatt is enamored with creation. He is bound to that innocent sense of wonder in which every new shade of color, blade of grass, and flicker of light captures his imagination. I'm convinced that somehow the God of this spellbinding creation is whispering words of romance and delight into his deepest soul.

But I don't hear them. I'm bored. I've seen plenty of twigs and frogs and ripples in the pond. I'm not so easily amused. I need more. Like Israel, God has become small to me. I'm disconnected from awe. I've lost the ability to lie under the stars and gasp. I'm addicted to *more*, and I miss the beauty of what sits directly in front of me.

Some of the truest things, the deepest things, are things we won't even see. We've looked at them every day, and we are numbed to their beauty. God's people said, "What have you done for us lately?"

Calloused, disinterested words leveled toward an ignored, dismissed lover.

The remainder of Malachi, the whole of Scripture, all the activity of God from time beginning to time ending answers this question. God has crafted galaxies and rumbled through history, shaped a people and fashioned a cross. God has gone to incredible lengths to pursue his own glory by winning the hearts of his people.

And these incredible lengths step outside our bounds, outside our sensibilities. In our world, grace and kindness equate with softness and gentleness. In our world, love usually means leniency, and the mention of forgiveness tends to arouse notions of a benign grandfather, kindly but removed, who dispassionately rocks away on his front porch.

No wonder we grow bored.

God is not a dispassionate Grandfather, a removed Deity, or an easily dismissed Lover. God knew that his people, lulled to the dangerous edges of apathy, were in need of what C. S. Lewis called a severe mercy. This was no time for weakness. Gentleness was not the antidote for the poison they had drunk. There are moments when love should turn wild, when a fire should burn in the belly and the steely gaze of the eyes should hint to a barbaric passion ready to leap.

If Miska were to come home today and declare she was in love with another man and was considering whether or not to leave, what would a deep, alive love look like for me? There is a place for subtle poetry and well-timed roses, and there is a time for letting go and simply allowing another to follow destructive choices. This would not be one of those times. I would fight for her. I would boldly declare love to her. And truth be told, this other man would do best to take a little vacation, far away and under an assumed identity. The jungles of Ecuador might be good because I promise you, I'd go looking. That's a raw, alive, savage love.

Israel was in a similar place: bored, disinterested, and considering other lovers. This was not the time for sweet words or cute stories. It was time for a savage grace.

And God delivered.

He spoke of his utter destruction of the Edomites, leveling their homeland and handing it over to the jackals. This teased Israel's memory of a God they had forgotten. But the Edomites were not the only target of God's intense scrutiny. God declared to Israel that this same love—cursing and crushing and ravaging—would soon be pursuing them:

> *"If you do not listen, and if you do not set your heart to honor my name," says the LORD Almighty, "I will send a curse upon you, and I will curse your blessings. Yes, I have already cursed them, because you have not set your heart to honor me. Because of you I will rebuke your descendants; I will spread on your faces the offal from your festival sacrifices, and you will be carried off with it. And you will know that I have sent you this admonition so that my covenant with Levi may continue," says the LORD Almighty. "My covenant was with him, a covenant of life and peace, and I gave them to him; this called for reverence and he revered me and stood in awe of my name."*[8]

Harsh words, but the moment insisted on harsh love.

God was going to curse them, to crush them with love. The imagery he evokes is gritty, repulsive with its unsanitary filth and foul odor. He will rub the offal, the manure and internal waste of their altar sacrifices, on their faces.[9] He will grab the backs of their heads and shove their noses deep into the excrement. He will take the very symbol of their dance with other lovers and make them drink it to its bitter end. If this false worship, this gluttonous whoring, is what they think they want, God will allow them to gorge on it until it makes them puke. It's a savage love, and apparently there are times when it's the only way.

God's acrid pursuit was not to spite or to appease jealousy gone mad. It was all for love. He intended to win their hearts, even if it required inflicting pain. We might not recognize it, but some things are better than comfort, worth even enduring affliction. The embrace of perfect love is such a thing, perhaps the only such thing.

There are a few choices a person should never have to make. They seem so unnatural, so out of order. Yet the clarity with which they can be determined is startling. Such was the case for Aron Ralston. It had been five days since he had first crawled into the three-foot crevice, and it had been five days since an eight-hundred-pound boulder had pinned his arm between the jagged rocks of the remote Utah canyon. Without water for three days, this experienced mountaineer knew time was running out. No one knew specifically where he was hiking, and the chances of anyone finding him were remote.

His choice was brutally clear: cut off his arm or watch his final sunset alone. He made his decision, but the only blade he had was dull. So he leveraged his arm against the boulder, breaking his bones so he could slice through the tissue. Then Aron Ralston pulled out his pocketknife and over the next excruciating hour sawed off his right arm. When he finished, he applied a tourniquet, rigged his anchors to the slate rock wall, and rappelled nearly seventy feet down to the bottom of Blue John Canyon. He began the hike out, and three hours later, he met up with the rescue party. He had lost his arm, but he had saved his life. It was a savage choice, made rightly with a savage love for something more, something truer.[10]

With the conviction of a lover who refuses to be denied, God makes such choices. He loves viciously. Earlier, his viciousness had aimed its veracity at the Edomites, ones far from pristine innocence, who "because of the violence against [Israel would be] covered with shame . . . destroyed forever."[11] And then there were the Amalekites, who like other Canaanite nations had barbarically attacked Israel at its weakest moments and for centuries had hunted the Israelites down, the chosen people their prey. God's ire raged against those who oppressed his people.

But his ire would also rage against his beloved who spurned his romancing advances. It's what one does when all that truly matters is at stake, when the cards are dealt and winner takes all. God insisted on the one thing any true lover would. He said with his words and his actions, "You can love me, or you can hate me, but you will not dismiss me."

It is uncanny how this ravaging nature of God's love catches us off guard. Our faith is fixed on a paradoxical event where wrath and mercy are bound together. At one time, on one cross, we find two seemingly opposing virtues. We see infinite forgiveness, free grace, and arms open wide for all of us, the worst of us, even those of us who mock him. Yet we also see unmatched fury, a violence so hideous that we grimace and turn away. These are not competing ideals leveraging for control until one wins out. These are two faces of the same heart, a heart that bleeds with unending compassion and overflowing kindness.

At times it simply requires a mystery, a savage grace, for us to see it.

CHAPTER 2

the darker side of faith

Time after time, I have seen families and even whole communities unite in prayer for the recovery of a sick person, only to have their hopes and prayers mocked. I have seen the wrong people get sick, the wrong people hurt, the wrong people die young.

—RABBI HAROLD KUSHNER

All who do evil are good in the eyes of the LORD, and he is pleased with them . . . Where is the God of justice?

—MALACHI 2:17

ot long ago, I accompanied twenty college students to a prayer and worship gathering near Bells, Texas. Bells is a sleepy little ranch town in the northeastern corner of the Texas plains. Our destination was actually several miles outside of town, an expansive ranch where cottonwoods and coyotes owned the rolling hills.

For the next two and a half days, we would be camping, braving the elements, and worshiping God along with thousands of other college students from across the nation. Most of our group had never been to Texas before, and they started in early with sarcastic remarks about the inane Texas pride that insists everything in the Lone Star State is "bigger and better."

They had yet to experience a Texas storm.

Around dusk, dark clouds began to roll in, and as the first raindrops fell, we battened down the tents and packed away all our goods. What began as a moderate shower with a few flashy streaks of lightning soon morphed into a full-fledged battle of nature. Thunder crackled, then boomed, and then captured the entire sky with a fury. Frenzied rain pelted the ground, bouncing off the parched earth and growing in intensity until it was almost raining hail.

The angry storm unleashed its full rage with the wind. Whipping from every direction, the gales forced many of the tents to surrender, mine included. The rain fly flapped as if it were answering the bugler charge, and both my front and center poles collapsed. For a while, I sat cross-legged on the floor of my toppled quarters, wrestling my tent as I held it down to the earth with both arms stretched out in a futile attempt to stay dry.

When it appeared there was no respite in sight and I admitted to myself that I couldn't keep up the fight for the entire night, I exited my sagging, dilapidated failure of a tent. I stood up, lightning illuminating our decimated campsite for a few seconds with each flickering volley. Taking the pummeling torrents head-on, I raised my fists to the manic, incandescent sky. Feeling the rage of Lieutenant Dan in *Forrest Gump*, I yelled to the winds, "Is that the best you have? Bring it on!"

I must have looked quite foolish, but somehow it brought levity to the camp. When the next pause in the storm came, we all fixed our tents, readjusting rain flies and driving in fresh stakes. The night was long, and the storm was unrelenting. By morning, the jabs at Texas egotism were silent.

On that second day, three more from our group joined us. They had missed the war with the elements, and so they sauntered into camp fresh and cheery. One of them, a freshman named James, had never been camping before, had never spent a night in a tent. He was already a little nervous about the proposition because roughing it wasn't his idea of a restful getaway, and his eyes widened as he heard our tales about the previous night.

James' nervousness turned to trepidation when we told him the weather forecast for that night: more of the same, only worse. Apparently, they were saying the previous wave was only a warm-up for what was to come.

With firm determination and more than a little concern, James demanded, "No, it will not rain. Claim it by faith. It will not rain. It will not rain." At first, I thought he was joking, mixing a little God-humor into a slightly testy situation. He wasn't. James was serious. It wasn't going to rain, and faith was going to make it so.

Immediately, my cynicism kicked in, and I thought, *Well, I just hope you have a sturdy tent because tonight, you're definitely going to need it.* Hearing the certainty of the gloomy forecast, I knew that despite his faith, James was in for an interesting night. There was even a bit of me eager to see him brave the chaos. It wasn't because of the storm, per se, but because a part of me I am ashamed of expected his faith, his certainty in God's actions, to be taken down a notch — just as mine has been so many times.

It wasn't to be. Around dusk, the weather patterns changed, and the sky turned crisp and clear. Faintly chirping mockingbirds replaced the thunder. Instead of hurling winds, there was a serene calm, and rather than lightning, celestial lights dotted the sky.

Chalk one up to faith, believing and seeing hope come to pass.

The next night, we began our long trek back to South Carolina. Our plans were to drive through the night, and I had the first shift. After four shots of Starbucks double espresso, I was wide-awake. I led our caravan with a van, and I had been chatting with another of our drivers on our radio for a couple of hours when I saw the lights flashing on the fast-approaching cruiser. He pulled in behind me, and I steered the van to the shoulder.

The officer told me he had clocked me at seventy-six miles per hour, normally not a speed that would warrant being stopped. However, he informed me that I had committed an egregious offense: I had sped through a construction zone. It was 3:30 a.m., not a normal hour for construction crews on duty. Furthermore, as I looked around, I saw no orange construction markers, signs, or any indications of roadwork.

I took the ticket, which included a two-hundred-dollar fine, and called the court the next day. I spoke to a kindly woman in the judge's office and explained my situation. She offered me several options for taking care of the ticket and said she would mail me the details. I don't know why, but for some reason I had a sense that the ticket would be taken care of. She didn't make any indication of this, but she knew we were a church group — and God knew I didn't have two hundred dollars to spare. Somehow I began to believe — maybe just hope — that she would have a change of heart, that she would wad up the ticket and forget it ever happened. I would claim it by faith.

Four days after arriving home, I went to the mailbox and found a nicely packed envelope from the judge's office in Waskom, Texas. Inside was all the appropriate documentation for me to comply with the terms of the ticket and pay the two hundred dollars.

This is the sort of experience with faith I am accustomed to: believing and being disappointed.

Faith is a tricky affair. On its hooks, we hang our dreams and aspirations. Faith demands we lay bare our deepest longings, our hidden and even forgotten desires. It kindles the embers of what we secretly want but have never dared to believe in, never dared to think could possibly come to life.

And then, almost without thought, it seems to follow a cruel, random path. For one, faith yields its tantalizing fruit with a marriage or a job more satisfying than was hoped for. For another, faith yields nothing, a barren harvest of shattered fortunes, wrecked relationships, and mocking, naïve presumptions. One has faith, and the storm passes. Another has faith and is stuck with a two-hundred-dollar traffic ticket.

Perplexing questions such as these haunt my spiritual dogma. I cling to belief, but I must honestly admit that there are times when it seems sheer foolishness. Doesn't the randomness of God's activity hint that it might not be God at all? What I experience seems more like chance, like spinning the roulette wheel, than divine order.

Traffic tickets are measly concerns, but a friend with a one-year-old son dying of leukemia isn't. I pray for small things, to be sure, and I could handle it if these prayers were rarely answered. I could even handle it if most of my large requests went unheeded. However, I can't think of the last time when I received some divine answer, some appeasement to my faith, that couldn't be explained by some other means: fate, arbitrary events, or simple cause and effect.

Why is it that when I feel most desperate, most estranged from God, most in need of intervention, God seems the farthest away? C. S. Lewis asked similar questions after his wife lost her battle with cancer:

> *Meanwhile, where is God? This is one of the most disquieting symptoms. When you are happy, so happy that you have no sense of needing Him . . . you will be — or so it feels — welcomed with open arms. But go to Him when your need is desperate, when all other help is vain, and what do you find? A door slammed in your face, and a sound of bolting and double bolting on the inside. After that, silence. You may as well turn away. The longer you wait, the more emphatic the silence will become. . . . Why is He so present a commander in our time of prosperity and so very absent a help in time of trouble?*[1]

Malachi spoke to a people whose cynicism conveyed their frustration with God's erratic behavior. Bothered by the affluence of those who denounced God, they accused God of losing control. As those who remained faithful to the covenant barely got by and those who flaunted their wickedness prospered with excess, the people fumed. Their words reeked with disappointment, and their angrily mumbled words were, "God, you are nowhere to be found. Your supposed justice is nothing but a joke."[2]

Who could blame them? Hadn't the covenant promised plenty — plenty of rain, plenty of crops, plenty of joy? Wasn't their end of the bargain to be faithful in following God's commands? Wasn't God's responsibility simple: to respond with timely deliveries of blessing? Simple.

But God wasn't coming through.

Like them, we struggle because of how faith has been defined for us. We have been told that faith is claiming a reality and seeing it come to pass. Faith is taking God at his word and waiting until we see him move. With varying terms and nuances, the oft-accepted notion of faith is that it is the means to aid us in seeing what God is doing so we can navigate the brief treacherous waters before we experience the hoped-for reality—here and now—that our faith claimed and clung to.[3]

The difficulty with criticizing such notions is that they mesh with much of Scripture. Christ boldly declared that faith as small as a tiny mustard seed would be enough to hurl a mountain into the sea. Hebrews 11, the defining text on faith, opens up with lofty talk of being "sure" and "certain," ideals seeming to promote an ironclad and well-forged resolve to never doubt, never question, never mutter under our breath seething words of disappointment.

As we peruse the examples Hebrews gives of the faithful ones, grand stories of triumphant faith cascade over the pages.

Abel, without any apparent experience in offering sacrifices, went against his brother's suggestion and in faith offered God the prime of his bounty. The result was immediate commendation from God. Faith delivered.

Enoch lived righteously, and before the ravages of old age claimed him, he was miraculously transported to heaven. Faith delivered.

Noah withstood the mocking neighbors and endured the long dismantling of his reputation. For years, he suffered the neighbors' insults of "kook" and "crazy man" because he believed, in faith, that the storms would come. And they came. Noah was the insane prophet no more. Faith delivered.

Abraham believed God told him to pack up his family and all he owned and embark on a journey to an unknown destination. He obeyed, and he began to see the nation he would father sprout before his final breath. Sarah haltingly believed the impossible — that a withered woman could bear a child — and her waning years were spent cuddling her son. Moses left Egypt to wander the desert and in faith returned to lead his haggard people out of that country. And lead them he did, unleashing frogs and locusts on their enemies, parting waters, and calling streams from a rock. Faith delivered and delivered and delivered again.

These stories were part of the history of Malachi's people. Hebrews, though written after Malachi, was simply a recollection of the same stories Malachi would have told, the same illustrations of faith Malachi would have given. Their history fueled a taut expectation of a bold faith with God arriving on the scene in miraculous ways. They were recent descendants of the faith heroes who adventured into these bold tales. In their own time, they had watched God bring them out of harsh captivity, seen the walls of Jerusalem rebuilt, and witnessed what for decades had been only a dream: a return to temple worship.

I have never seen faith deliver in such magnificent fashion. My faith is far more complicated. Soured by sizable faith-endeavors that never came through, I have settled into hoping for smaller things: a decent parking spot or the chance to catch a foul ball at the ballpark. Some might dismiss such requests as trivial or sacrilegious. Perhaps they are, but they result not from some catty opportunity to mock faith but from years of deflated hopes. Having to park in the back lot of the mall is far less disquieting than watching my lifelong dream dissipate.

Faith is a call to hope. It entices us to believe again, to stare our disillusionment in the face and grab on for another round. Faith is dangerous, and for most of us, we've had enough, thank you. Perhaps our sputtering faith results from a skewed reading of the history of God's people and God's movement. The distortion is inflicted on us when our notion of faith — believing something into reality *now* — grows into a demand. This is how faith *always* works, how faith *must* work.

A continued reading of Hebrews offers a much less ambitious, much less romantic foray into faith than its readily quoted portions. Following the adventurous and acclaimed bunch rattled off in the heroic listing, a much more somber docket is offered. In stark contrast to the saber-rattling, swashbuckling tales of those who rushed off with God into the darkness and emerged on the other side flush with triumph and hungry for more, we find an unnamed and innumerable catalog of affliction.

Here we read of the many who were not lifted to heaven, did not lead Israel into a lauded victory, did not see the waters part, and did not cross the Jordan on dry ground. They did not see their children raised from the dead, were not delivered from their final earthly moment of torture and agony, and never saw any relief from their wounds or despair.

Rather, they were granted, while clinging to faith, the opportunity to be cast into a Roman cage as gladiators, to be stripped naked and hung in the public courts, and to be driven from their homes to wander in search of shelter. They saw their children raped and their wives ripped apart by wild dogs. All the while, they were fiercely holding on to faith.[4]

Such stories make me squirm. Who is this God I thought I knew? One moment he sends a pillar of fire so his people can navigate the Judean terrain, and the next moment he sits idly by as torture chambers echo with a child's cry, a child desperately grasping on to faith. These memories knock a bit of the luster off my polite and ambitious demands. They raise more questions than answers. They might actually foster a fresh stirring of genuine, God-centered, heaven-directed faith.

I have regularly used faith as my means to make God move, to get what I want. I am tenaciously addicted to making my life work. God is often the means to an end rather than the end. He is the One I pay dutiful homage to with the clear expectation that he will come through when he is supposed to. I expect him to make my life manageable and comfortable, if not easy and successful. I expect him to provide the job I want, keep my wife and boys safe, and provide a few perks along the way, such as a trip to Alaska or a pair of jet skis. I do my part by being a faithful follower, and he does his part by removing at least most of the larger obstacles and bringing me to the end of my days so I can pass away my golden years reclining comfortably in my La-Z-Boy.

We often approach God as a means to get what we want, but his desire is to in fact *be* what we want. We ascribe to what Larry Crabb has termed the "principle of linearity."[5] Much like Job's misguided friends, we believe that physical blessing is a sign of a well-lived life, while experiences that go awry signal a disobedient life. Supposedly, it's a clear and well-attested formula: Live faithfully and receive great blessing; live unfaithfully and suffer great toil. Simple. Easy. It works.

Until you pray for months for the safety of your expected child, and in the seventh month, another miscarriage wrecks your heart. Until you pray for your marriage, spending countless hours in counseling and begging God for mercy, and she still leaves without even so much as a glance of regret. Until you spend years modeling faithfully, though imperfectly, to your children what it means to be a God-follower, believing with all the faith you can muster that they too will embrace your God, but they don't. They walk away and never return.

Our fellow travelers in Hebrews know this terrain well. The poignant conclusion to their disturbing stories echoes with an eerie ring: "These were all commended for their faith, yet *none of them received what had been promised.*"[6]

A more careful reading of the earlier portion of Hebrews 11, where the grand and courageous accounts are delivered, would have pointed us toward a similar place, which is curious in light of the vastly contrasted direction of their lives. After rambling through the tales of Abel, Enoch, Noah, and Abraham and Sarah, the writer interjects, "All these people were still living by faith when they died. *They did not receive the things promised.*"[7]

God didn't come through.

I feel misguided, lied to. This is an angle on faith I never heard in my church's children's classes. I haven't read of it in many popular Christian devotional books. From the vantage point I have been led to, God always comes through. What God promises, he delivers.

Maybe I should temper my indignation. Maybe I heard what I wanted to hear. The far less complicated version of faith is much more to my liking. It makes God indebted to me. Subtly, it makes me larger than him.

It fits in rather nicely with the course I have mapped out for myself filled with objectives, goals, and agendas. With my career, if I apply a good work ethic and stay focused, I am certain to achieve a level moderately close to my targeted spot on the totem pole. With my family, if I provide a nice house and consistent care sprinkled with proper doses of quality time, it should achieve its desired effect. In my marriage, a good bit of tenderness mixed with an ample supply of affection, all smothered by well-tuned listening skills, should surrender a contented and at times even exciting string of anniversaries.

It all works out so nicely. Everything in its place, and all working out just as planned. And why should my spiritual journey be any different? I do my part, and God does his. Faith is the cog that keeps the divine wheel oiled and rolling. It's really quite a beautiful setup.

Until it wrecks. The wheel comes spinning off, and our life careens toward the guardrail hugging the edge of a precipice. God doesn't work for us anymore. The truth is, he never did.

Most of the larger theological questions about God really are camouflage hiding much fiercer personal fears we are desperate to hold at bay. The question of theodicy, how a good God could allow evil in the world, has baffled philosophers and theologians since their disciplines were formed. While it might be an interesting theoretical question, the stinging agony of this question oozes from horrendous personal tragedy when the faith we have known and been weaned on disintegrates.

Rabbi Harold Kushner, writing from the backdrop of the holocaust inflicted on his people, says it most bluntly: "There is only one question which really matters: why do bad things happen to good people? . . . Virtually every meaningful conversation I have ever had with people on the subject of God and religion has either started with this question, or gotten around to it before long."[8]

What disturbs me most about this question is, sadly, not so much my sorrow over the unspeakable pain others face but rather the haunting reality that if they are not safe, neither am I. Since our wedding day, Miska has faced fears that I would die, leaving her alone in the world. There are months when her fear rarely surfaces, but there are days when it holds her in a strangling grip of dread. I used to respond to her with a tight hug and warm assurance: "I won't die. Everything will be fine. I promise." On one such day, she replied, "Don't say that you promise. You can't say that. You don't know."

She was right. I don't know. I don't know if all my dreams of taking my sons on a trek across Denali National Forest or on a river rampage through the Grand Canyon will materialize—I don't know if I'll be around that long. I don't know if I'll see my sons marry and make their mark in the world. I don't know if I will die a contented and aged man in the comforts of my home, having lived long and well. I don't know.

Far worse than the prospect of my own premature passing, I don't know that my sons will outlive me. I don't know that my wife will be by my side, as I plan, for the decades to come. I just don't know. Wish as I might, believe as I do, I can't say for sure.

In the critically acclaimed film *The Pianist*, the story of Wladyslaw Szpilman's survival during Poland's Nazi occupation, these disturbing questions emerge at every turn. Every story of the Holocaust tears at my sense of humanity and decency, but now that I'm a father, this story has become more personal. As I watched the scenes of the Polish Jews being herded into small, fenced-in plots, heard the wails of children, and saw the little girl, probably five or six, in a daze, desperately scanning the mob of people for her mom, I winced and grimaced at the affliction.

Then there was the woman holding her limp son who looked to be two or three years old, frantically rushing from person to person and begging for a drop of water for him because he was dying of thirst. Soon after this, Miska had to leave the room. Watching such carnage was hard enough for her before becoming a mom, but now, the questions it raises and the possibilities it invokes are simply too much to take.

Where was God in all of this?

These people did not deserve such evil any more than I do. These parents did not have any smaller hopes or any fewer dreams for their children than I do. Their hopes, their dreams, their honest and moral lives—their faith—did not spare them from such terror. In times I'd rather ignore and in moments I'd rather dismiss, I must admit that my faith does not guarantee me any safer path.

And it is the safe path that I am vehemently committed to. I want to believe there is some pattern I can follow with meticulous care, some moral guide or set of principles I can invest in with rigorous devotion that would ensure the desired result: comfort and success. I desire a prayer I can repeatedly pray or a discipline I can dutifully perform that will yield me assurance and constancy.

Yet the further I plunge into these pursuits, the more I am thwarted by my desires. It seems the more desperately I need to hear God, the more distant he is. I often find that when I think I have been most faithful and deserve the most blessing, trouble hovers, and when I have strayed farther and been less mindful of God, blessings often abound.

God seems to do whatever he pleases with little regard for my schemes, and that is utterly disconcerting. How can it be? Doesn't our humanity scream at us that people get what they deserve? That if we live well and love others, our lives will turn for the better, and if we are evil and disdain goodness, our lives will turn for the worse? Our humanity might suggest such notions, but our reality at times doesn't bear them out.

Kushner shared such unsettling thoughts: "Time after time, I have seen families and even whole communities unite in prayer for the recovery of a sick person, only to have their hopes and prayers mocked. I have seen the wrong people get sick, the wrong people hurt, the wrong people die young."[9]

These honest words disturb me: "the wrong people." There are some who deserve evil, and there are some who don't. The line seems clear, and it should never be crossed. But it is crossed all the time, and I don't know what to do with that. I don't know what that says about my God, and I don't know what that says about the way I have been taught to live my life, full of faith and confidence that the guys in the white hats always walk away with the pretty girls in the end.

So I continue to grasp and tussle with my fears. I want to be assured that I know how to operate with the Almighty. I want to know that when I need him, when I really need him, he will come through. I want to believe that somehow there is a way to harness him, a way to make faith work. I will do anything to hold on to my illusion that I can manage my life. I will deny any reality or cling to any principle that keeps God indebted to my bidding. I must stay in control, and I must hang on to my ability to maneuver and manipulate.

If faith is the only way, then I will grind deeper, run faster, and believe harder. I will make faith work. I will *make God work.*

But I have found that no amount of faith can offer me such a guarantee. There is no way to ensure that God will deliver what I expect. The bitter reality is that often God is a God who disappoints.

In our darkest moments, the human struggle is to hold on to hope.

Hope, however, is a painful exercise. Merely the attempt opens up the terrifying possibility that we will be disappointed. The worst is when it is God who does the disappointing.

This is why mystery terrifies me. It rips back the curtain and reveals that I am the wizard pulling strings and blowing whistles, frantically grabbing at life. I am desperate to keep the curtain closed, desperate to hold on to the little bit of pseudoreality I have carved out for myself. It might be denial, but it's safe.

How do I handle a God who does what he wills when he wills? How do I manage a God who might respond to my obedience with a pay raise but just as easily might respond with a pink slip? How do I maneuver around a God who makes absolutely no guarantees about the safety of my family or the certainty of achieving what I have committed my life to?

I don't. I can't, and that is the beautifully treacherous allure of mystery.

CHAPTER 3

stepping into the story

It was in fairy-stories that I first divined the potency of the words, and the wonder of the things.

—J. R. R. TOLKIEN

That is the object of the story, to arouse wonder in us.

—ELIE WIESEL

Have we not all one Father? Did not one God create us?

—MALACHI 2:10

Sometimes preaching can be a hideously frightening endeavor. On some Sundays, I stand up, open my Bible, and look out to see all the faces, expectant expressions from many I know and love and gazes of anticipation from many I wouldn't recognize if we bumped into each other downtown or at the market. As I stand there before these faces, I realize an unnerving reality: These people — at least most of them — are actually listening to me. I am not quite so self-inflated as to believe they hang on my every word or blithely take my ramblings as gospel. But they *are* there. They are, for the most part, listening.

I wonder what exactly it is they are listening to. What could I possibly have to say? It's just me standing up there, offering an untidy mix of wisdom and foolishness. I am no different from the rest of us—confused child, bold prophet, lonely soul, lover of God all jumbled up together. Depending on when you catch me, you will have different takes on who I am. Some moments you will think saint, but in other, perhaps more frequent moments, all you will see is sinner. And so on days when I'm feeling my sin more acutely or my doubt more vividly, I wonder to myself as I stand and the faces look on, *If they knew the unease in my soul, would the room empty faster than it filled?* Is it just a spiritually veiled arrogance when I wonder how many would still listen if they knew the real me? Is my neurosis evidenced merely by my asking?

There is a humbling reality to these questions, and I need to be asking them, perhaps regularly. I need to own up to the gravity of standing before God's people and claiming to offer God's message. There is integrity in remembering that it is possible for God's words to be lost amid my vocabulary, for God's speaking to be muted by my increased volume.

As a pastor, is my primary job to deliver my message, my insights, or my most recent discoveries from the scriptural text? Is what *I* have to say foremost? I wonder if my attempts to preach to a modern world have grown a little too modern and, for all its relevance and interaction with our new realities, the actual preaching (speaking again what God has already spoken) has become obscured.

If God has intervened in human history and spoken, and if God's people throughout this long history have practiced the collective art of listening, struggling to hear and obey what it was he said, then my arrival on the stage on any given Sunday is of minor significance. Little of my task in preaching centers on me: my ingenious interpretations, my insightful observations, or my skillfully placed application. If God and his people have been hearing and speaking to each other for centuries, then the largest portion of my job in preaching is simply to recount the conversation.

This radically reorients my view of my given role. I am less the entrepreneurial explorer, launching into uncharted territory, and more the family storyteller. I am the one who helps the next generation remember the long procession of those who have come before them. The history of previous generations is their history. Histories are not re-created; they are simply reentered, reexperienced.

When I stand to open God's Word, the account of God's speaking through history, the authority present is not an authority I *bring* to the moment but an authority I *join* in that moment. The authority does not emerge from me, but rather, as I stand under the text, kneeling before the Trinity, and in humility submitting to the witness of God's people throughout history, this is God's moment. These are God's words. These are the collected stories of God's people. I am just helping us remember.

Will Willimon retells the story of a young pastor of a small church who faced a snooty parishioner one Sunday after the service. As she passed him on her way out, she muttered something about his tender age of thirty, wondering how he could possibly claim to know anything at all. Willimon tells how "her pastor drew himself up to his full height, clutched the stole around his neck, and said, 'Madame, when I wear this and I climb into that pulpit, I am over two thousand years old, and speak from two millennia of experience.'" [1]

There might have been some arrogance in this pastor's response, but his point is well taken. In fact, it comforts me. When we gather as God's people each and every Sunday, we are participating in the ancient practice of remembering, retelling, and embracing the story of God and his dealings with his people.

My preaching isn't about me. It is about my very human — and often muddled — attempts to recast God's interactions with his people from the opening pages of Genesis up to today. Our worship — the music sung and the gospel read and the peace passed and the prayers offered — isn't about us, our devotion, or our faithfulness. It is about God. It is about remembering God's devotion to himself and to his people through the annals of history. It is about God's faithfulness to be who he says he is each time he speaks. It is about our collective grasping for faithfulness during the long times of silence between God's vocal moments.

For me, the purpose of corporate worship has shifted. I see it less as a time constructed to expound new truths from Scripture or as an opportunity to embrace the spiritual discipline of public devotion to God. I see it more as a moment when we as God's people actually step into our roots, when we enter God's story. It is our moment to step onto God's stage, the moment when we become actors in God's drama.

In entering God's production, we hold our own copies of the script, and our ears practice the art of listening, bent toward hearing the cues for our turn to speak, our turn to act, our turn to obey. God's story becomes more than static history; it becomes living history. God's story becomes our story, not through unengaged recollecting, but by diving in, being drenched in the current reality and the present experience.

This is mystery.

This is the beauty of liturgy. Liturgy means "the work of the people."[2] Some dismiss liturgy as cold, dead ritualism (and like any spiritual activity, it is certainly possible to settle for the form rather than the spirit), but it is a mistake to so easily surrender something God's people through the ages have participated in as a visible means of entering God's narrative.

The church I pastor belongs to a strange breed. We are difficult to label. We like to describe ourselves with artistic, clever words such as *eclectic*. Others would think of more suitable, less self-serving words, I'm sure. Many churches that refer to themselves as liturgical would be offended if we did the same. We are probably less refined and almost certainly a whole lot messier.

The last meeting space we had was a converted warehouse where after every rain, small Tupperware bowls were strategically placed in the large meeting room to catch predictable drips from the leaking roof. The walls were painted ruby plum, and our space designated for coffee and conversation — the Bean Room — rarely offered Starbucks. *Folgers is considerably cheaper*, we would remind ourselves.

Our band never shies away from old-fashioned rock 'n' roll, and on many Sundays they can be found offering their own rendition of Dave Matthews or Ani DiFranco. Even our order of worship has been given its own twist — our worship leader has dubbed it the Sundae Scoop.

A few weeks ago, a man stopped me before the Sunday service. "I just want you to know," he said, "that you deliver a hell of a sermon." He didn't flinch. He didn't crack a smile, some mischievous clue that he had used a word he really wasn't supposed to. He just kept shaking my hand to make sure I'd heard what he said: "hell of a sermon."

We're a messy group.

At the same time, our journey over the past few years has moved us away from trying so hard to be fresh, to be relevant. There was a time when we were the "cool church," the place to go to hear something new — or at least something old said in a way you had never heard it before. We were the place to get loud, get rowdy, and do it in God's name.

We were rebels. We were the church that was antichurch. No robes here (not to mention ties or khakis), no organs or dreary hymns. None of that formal religious stuff. We were the church that was actually fun to attend.

Somewhere along the way, it began to feel empty, void of depth. We were enjoying ourselves, but somehow in our attempts to be fresh and relevant, we had managed to create an experience that was exactly that: an experience we had created. It was loud, but it didn't evoke awe. The teaching was current, but it rarely baffled us. We had strategies and plans, but we didn't have much transcendence. We had a crowd and a good bit of success, but we didn't have much mystery. We began to see worship as our entrance into God's story rather than our attempts to get him to step into ours. Rather than being so preoccupied with looking forward, we began to look back. We began to look for our roots, to ask questions about our heritage. We began to ask what Christians did to embrace and encounter their God long before we arrived on the scene with our new paradigms and our never-thought-of-before slants on the faith.

Little that we changed was dramatic, and none of it was flashy. It was all quite simple. Sharing communion was already a regular part of our culture, but it took on fresh meaning. We have come to see the weekly breaking of the bread and drinking of the wine as a sacred moment when we gather as one community around the Lord's table, sharing the Lord's meal. We share a common cup because we share a common God, a common history, a common story.

Each week, we set aside time to pass to one another the peace of Christ. It is an intimate time when the Spirit of Christ in one greets the Spirit of Christ in another. There are handshakes, hugs, and even tears. It is a moment when we believe Christ lives in our words. Somehow in ways we cannot quite describe, God's very presence is offered to one another as we pass the simple greeting, "Peace of Christ to you."

At some point in our public worship, usually toward the beginning, a portion of the gospel is read. Following the common lectionary each week, another piece of the story of Christ is read aloud. We introduce the reading with plain yet weighty words: "This is the gospel, the Word of God, the story of Christ and our hope." We do this every Sunday. I could imagine a Sunday without preaching, without music, perhaps even without coffee and donuts before we began, but I could never imagine a Sunday without the gospel being read. The gospel is the story of Christ, the story of God. If we are truly God's people as we say we are, then the gospel is our story. Somehow when we hear the stories retold of how Christ healed, how he spoke, how he taught, we hear and see and taste our own history.

We are also attempting to live more in line with the calendar of the church. Following the standard schedule of Advent, Epiphany, Lent, the Resurrection, and Pentecost, we are declaring that all things, even time, are centered on God. We are declaring that history is God's, our days are God's, and we are God's. Gatherings such as our Maundy Thursday service are a focal point of our fellowship as we remember

God's intervention in history, remember his words, remember his actions, remember him.

The power of these simple, old rites of the church is that they are tactile. The bread settles on the tongue, and the wine trickles down the back of the throat. The word *peace* is whispered, and the flesh and bones of the one doing the embracing are connected to the flesh and bones of the one being embraced. Such ancient acts have formed the church's worship as long as our memories can stretch. They did not dig their way into our tradition simply because we are creatures of routine. They became part of the texture of our worship because they represent the heart of what the church's corporate worship is: telling, remembering, and entering God's story.

Even the mere fact of gathering on Sunday is a gateway into God's narrative. As we gather on the first of the week, we are joining centuries of other Sunday gatherers. Though we might be tempted to believe otherwise, the Sunday gathering is not a mere social invention. Certainly, in some places there has been a strong cultural element connected with the supposed Sabbath. In the Texas of my youth, blue laws kept anyone from buying beer on Sunday. So Saturday nights from eleven to midnight saw an exorbitant level of liquor purchases. Even where I currently live in South Carolina, stores can sell only food items on Sundays until 1:00. No beer, of course, but also no automotive supplies, no Liquid Plumber, no toothbrushes. Apparently the Sabbath has been shortened to thirteen hours, but they still like to respect it.

The reality, however, is that we gather on the first day of the week because on one dark, depressing Sunday morning, Jesus rose from the dead. Light erupted. Life broke free. Stunned, the apostles and the witnesses of Christ's resurrection ignited a movement in which people for two millennia have gathered on Sundays to remember what happened. To tell the story. To experience it for themselves.

All of these corporate acts of worship are realities we experience, not forms we control. When we forget that we are a story-entering and story-telling community and that our rites and traditions and preaching are invitations to step onto the stage, then the story ebbs, our hearts grow cool, and church becomes only a gathering to decipher the story rather than live it.

And many in the church have become fantastic decoders, mining all the details of the story. We craft biographical sketches of the leading characters. We create a time line for the major events. We chart the plot and even memorize many of the lines. But somehow, despite all this, we never actually put on a costume. We never place ourselves in the story, submitting to its flow and emotion.

In high school, I was in drama. We were a small school. And when I say small, I mean really small. My graduating class boasted the proud number of twelve, the number of Christ's disciples, I assured myself. With such few people to choose from, those of us who really wanted to get involved were given more than ample opportunity.

One year, I was given the part of Scrooge in the annual Christmas play. I was actually the backup Scrooge, but a month before we were scheduled to perform, the original Scrooge was kicked out of school. I think the school administration must have found out what had happened to Tiny Tim.

I had read a little of Dickens, and who didn't know the story of *The Christmas Carol*? But I tell you, as small and low-budget as our production was, it came alive for me. I immersed myself in the character.

I hunched over, spoke in a gravelly voice, and felt myself descending into the dark world Dickens had created.

In strange ways, I no longer controlled the story, but it controlled me. My character took on a life of its own. I experienced greed and pride and fear in ways I never could have experienced in the normal, controlled fashion of unengaged reflection or moralistically styled research.

I once heard about a prominent Christian author who baptized himself each morning as an act of cleansing from sin and a way to set himself apart to God for that day. I don't know if it is true or not, but I like the idea. It seems to me that playing a Dickens character, baptizing yourself daily, or breaking the bread and the wine are all forms of the same experience: abandoning yourself to something beyond yourself, surrendering to One who refuses to be controlled but rather insists on doing the controlling.

Stories move us. They invite us to enter in, to be led along, to experience. Stories open up new vistas and introduce us to strange worlds and wild, quirky characters. Stories remind us of things long forgotten. Stories swallow us up.

In stories, we do not control the characters, the plot, or the outcome. We cannot change a romance gone sour or the disturbing fact that the villain is winning the day. If we are immersed in it, we are at the story's mercy.

Stories are more than a genre, more than a singular category in the broad scope of various art forms. Stories are a context, a way of seeing. Stories form reality. A painter might brush a world onto a canvas, but a story forms what the painter sees, the realm from which he works and creates.

Stories are textured. They shift and move. They contain facts, yet they could never be defined merely as a collection of data. They often provide commentary or critique, yet they should never be misunderstood as simply tools for craftily nuanced analysis. Stories often contain these elements — and more — but they are not defined by them. Stories actually define the world around them. Stories use everything at their disposal — wit, conviction, tragedy, horror, irony — to create a world.

It is sad when we lose sight of our collective stories and forget what formed us, what made us who we are. It is a tragedy when we neglect what Wendy Wright has reminded us to do: "to heed the *sensus fidelium* (the collective sense of the faithful)."[3]

Stories have always been core to humanity. Each culture, regardless of time or geography, has told stories. In a world where words — the printed page and the talking-saturated mediums — have ravenously gobbled up our attention, it is easy to forget that words are only functions of a much larger reality: stories.

The earliest cultures passed along their reality — their view of and experience with the world — as stories in picture form. Ancient cave drawings and barely preserved parchments remind us that the earliest communication might have been crude with its stick people and one-dimensional texture, but it was alive with passion and intrigue, romance and deceit. Kingdoms were raised up, emperors were thrown down, and entire cultures were remembered and mythologized by rudimentary carvings made with flint on stone and simple sketches drawn with charcoal on sheepskin. Each culture since has kept its memory alive by passing on to the next generation its stories of family feuds, political upheavals, joys and conquests and mishaps. We call it history.

We might not recognize it, but stories define our world. Politics is little more than competing stories, conflicting attempts to describe what has happened in the world and how the plot should turn next. Cultural religion is man's best stab at giving depth to the story, describing who the main characters are and what the moral of the story might be. Marketing is the never-ending effort to write new stories after making us tired or disinterested in the old. Science often scoffs at our naïve, outdated stories and replaces them with newer, shinier ones that will in turn be naïve and outdated next year. Philosophy questions if there really is such a thing as meaning to the story, then questions if there really is such a thing as story, then gets really perplexed when it questions if there really is such a thing as questions. You get the idea.

Despite their persistent presence, we often lose sense of these stories. We allow them to hum in the background, but we often neglect to give them their place, to pull up a chair and listen to their truth, their wisdom. We take them for granted, forget the way they form us. Tragically, we often abandon the story's central feature. We forget the Author. We forget God. And we push the stories away.

Yet something inside us resists. Stories are written into our soul.

My son Wyatt has begun the habit of repeating the details of his recent encounters, events, or conversations. He mumbles them to himself. He yells them at a neighbor. He tells them to his nine-month-old brother, Seth, who listens with kind attention. He regularly repeats them for his mom and me.

Wyatt doesn't even talk in complete sentences yet. His conversation is a concentrated string of words connected in a cute and often comically innovative way. Still, he persistently fights his way through the hard work of making sure he communicates what he wants us to hear, what he wants us to remember.

A recent misadventure occurred when he opened up the refrigerator, pulled out the egg carton, and spilled the dozen eggs out onto the hardwood floor. Referring to himself in third person as he does, for days we heard, "Wyatt . . . eggs . . . floor." Only three words, but those three words contained a story of curiosity and an escapade turned messy.

This weekend, I had to be away for a retreat. As I walked out the front door with my bags, I stopped and gave Wyatt a hug, telling him I would come back home soon. When I called Miska on Friday night, she told me that Wyatt had been repeating a three-word phrase all afternoon and evening. He told it to Miska. He told it to the babysitter who played with him for a couple of hours while Miska was out. Wyatt's three-word mantra was, "Daddy . . . comin' . . . home." It was important to him to remember, to place his immediate story in the larger context. Daddy was gone, but it wouldn't always be so. He found it necessary to repeat the rest of the story, as if it gave him hope: "Daddy . . . comin' . . . home."

From someplace deep in his soul, Wyatt knows he lives in stories. He knows that stories allow us to remember. Already, Wyatt is showing that he belongs to a race of storytellers.

The Scripture as a whole is a story. Certainly this is true on a surface level with over two-thirds of the biblical material being stories about God and people and people running away from God and God running after people. However, when we say that God speaks in stories, we mean something more. We mean that God is the great story maker. It isn't that God uses stories as a medium, simply a means to another end, or as support to bolster some profound truth he desires humans to grasp. God isn't a fiery preacher who knows just when to accentuate certain points with just the right illustration to get the desired effect. God thinks in story. God crafts story. God *is* story.

The truth is, God has really written only one story. It is a story that stretches as far back as human memory and looks as far forward as the end of all things. It remembers all God has done, and it anticipates all God has yet to do.

This one story is not all there is to God, but it is all God has chosen to reveal of himself to us. This one story is *the story*. It is all of God's movement toward humanity, all of God's revealed actions that have intersected with creation's history.

It is the magnificent telling of how God created those he would call his friends and how he gave to them all that was good. It tells how unexplainable choices were made in the Garden of Eden, how indescribable evil entered as a result, and how every moment since has been a colossal conflict between the one who deceived and the One who pursues. The story weaves through the tales of a people he loved who simply would not love back. It tells of a Carpenter called God, a cross, and a Resurrection. And it returns once again to the well-worn theme of a people he loved who simply would not love back.

This story is what we call gospel.

And God is still writing to us. Amazingly, he is even writing with us. This Great Story is pervasive and final, while at the same time not closed. It is all around us and deep within us. G. K. Chesterton saw this clearly. He believed that every good story was really only a retelling of the gospel.

So although God has spoken in words through prophets and divine Scripture, he has ultimately spoken beyond mere words with story. God's center moment of speaking was from Mount Sinai, where his thunderous voice rumbled out instructions for those who would call him God. His opening line was meant to reorient them to their true reality, their place in the ancient-present story of God. "I am the LORD your God, who brought you out of Egypt" was what he first offered.[4] He wanted them to remember that the story had not begun that morning as they woke the young and prepared for the day's task. The story had not begun in earlier weeks as they faced the raging heat and the constant search for water. The story pointed back to the activity of God, which he demonstrated by his miraculous intervention in pulling them out of bondage, and went back even much, much further than that. His reminder was that while this most certainly was their story, more than that, it was God's story.

Israel's prophets and sages often returned to the art of storytelling. Whenever Moses stood before the grumbling people, they expected a good round of stories reminding them of God's reality and how they fit into it. In the same way, Scripture is a collected record of the story of God. While there are many literary devices and genres, they all connect for the same purpose: to tell the story, God's story. As we immerse ourselves in its pages, we connect with its truth and find life, meaning. We find that Wright was correct when she told us "our lives are experienced as meaningful to the extent that they are undergirded by a narrative worthy of our dreams."[5]

God is a storytelling God, and because we are made in his image, we are a storytelling people. Elie Wiesel even suggested that God's motivation for creating mankind was because of his love for stories. To forget the form of story, to not allow it center stage, is to miss God.

This being true, the work of the people of God is to stay in the story, to dive into it, to experience it, to tell it, to live it. Our acts of public worship and private devotion, our working and loving and dying, our families and our vocations, our faith communities and our civic discourse — all of these are merely acts in the play, opportunities to step into the story.

This is the whole of Malachi's message: We are in God's story — he isn't in ours. The repentance he urged from Israel and the worship he called them to were opportunities to submit to and join in on God's narrative.

Yesterday I prayed the canticle for the twenty-ninth day from Robert Benson's collection of prayers called *Venite*. They are old prayers made up of old words and old theology. They have been prayed countless times across the bounds of history and geography. As I prayed, I allowed myself to enter into the prayer, to participate in the reality that this was the ancient confession of God's people — all of God's people. It wasn't from this year or this decade or even this century. It was a prayer emerging from the story of us all, the story of God.

As I read and prayed, my heart was released to worship. I paused at each break in the canticle as a deep stirring rose within me. My inner response follows each stanza of the canticle:

> *You are God: we praise You.*
> *You are the Lord: we acclaim You.*

These are the words God's people have spoken since the beginning of time. Since humanity first breathed on this earth, the faithful have proclaimed God's reality. This is not new. This is not modern. It is a declaration of faith, an old and well-worn faith.

You are the eternal One: And all creation worships You.
To You all angels, all powers of heaven,
    Cherubim and Seraphim, sing in endless praise:

God is outside my sensory experiences of reality. What is fanciful to me — heaven and angels and forces I cannot see or touch — is my issue, not God's. My small perceptions of reality do not limit him. If my faith falters, nature's faith does not. The created order knows what is true. This is what God's people long before me have always proclaimed.

Holy, holy, holy Lord, God of power and might,
heaven and earth are full of Your glory.
    The glorious company of apostles praise You,
    the noble fellowship of prophets praise You,
        the white-robed army of martyrs praise You.
Throughout the world the holy Church acclaims You:
    Father, of majesty unbounded;
Your true and only Son, worthy of all worship;
    and Holy Spirit, advocate and guide.

God's people, the company of the faithful, are as old as the age of human civilization. As long as there have been people walking on this planet, there have been people believing in the one God. Some have lived for it; some have died for it. The church crosses every boundary: chronological, geographical, racial, political, social, and economic. The church is all of God's people across all of time. I have arrived at the party late.

> *You, Christ, are the king of glory, the eternal*
> *Son of the Father.*
> *When You became man to set us free,*
> *You did not shun the Virgin's womb.*
> *You overcame the sting of death,*
> *and opened the kingdom of heaven to all believers.*
> *You are seated at God's right hand in glory.*
> *We believe that You will come and be our judge.*

God is beyond time. He is past, present, and future. He entered history, invading human time and space. All of time past echoes:

> *Come then, Lord, and help Your people,*
> *bought with the price of Your own blood,*
> *and bring us with Your saints, to glory everlasting.*[6]

Every generation has waited, longed, and hoped. Every generation has struggled to believe in something they do not see. Every generation has wondered if they might have been deluded, and in every generation, some have known they have not. God is. God died. God rose.

In this prayer, I stepped into my history. It was not a time for grammatical analysis or theological dissection. It was simply a time to gather around the kitchen table, worn with long years of meals shared, tears spilled, and faith believed, and to eat, to feast. Rational argument did not move me in this prayer. Doctrinal assent was not the fuel of my awakened heart. The life I felt stirring within me came when I merely rested in the words, allowing the pressure to *know* to dissipate while I experienced the joy of the family reunion.

This is mystery: experiencing something we cannot manipulate and abandoning ourselves to One we cannot control. Embracing mystery demands that we refuse to stand over our history, examining it and judging it with aloof, sterile detachment. Mystery takes it in like a child's first step onto the vast expanse of the white sands of the beach. Surrendering to the smells, the cool spray from the incoming tide, the warm sun, and the grainy coolness shifting under his feet, he simply enters into the ocean's world. The young heart has no way to know what it is he is dealing with; he simply has to dive in and feel it for himself.

Our histories, the stories that have shaped us, are a way of diving in. They give us a sense of ourselves. They stir something deep within us. They remind us that we are not the first to believe, the first to doubt, or the first to wonder who we are or what God could possibly be up to. They give us courage, and they show us our place as the latest additions to a long line of pilgrims struggling with faith.

Metropolitan Baptist Church in Washington, D.C., is an African American congregation with a rich sense of history. A century and a half ago, a small band of slaves huddled together. They were powerless, fearful, and plagued with uncertainty. The War between the States raged on, and their humanity—in many ways their permission to exist—hung in the balance.

As has been true for generations of God's people, they worshiped. It was all they knew to do. And decades later, to people who don't remember their names and live in a world they would never recognize, their story breathes courage. Dr. H. Beecher Hicks Jr., only the fifth senior minister of this historic congregation, spoke recently to his large flock. Facing heavy challenges and formidable hurdles in the life of the church, he began his address with a bit of history:

> One hundred and forty years ago, a few worn and weary sons and daughters of God, indelibly kissed by nature's sun, gathered for prayer and praise in the barracks of Quaker soldiers. To be sure, they were uncertain in their gathering. They were not certain of the outcome of the Civil War between the states. They were uncertain of their future. They were uncertain of life itself. They were certain, however, that the God who had brought them across the swelling waters of the Atlantic, the God who had been with them through the middle passage and sustained them through the sweltering cotton fields of the South would be the God who would keep them and provide for them and make a way for them through this new wilderness of hardship and pain. Literally living through "dangers, toils, and snare," residents of a place called "hell's bottom," they held on to their faith, they held on to hope unborn, they held on to each other.[7]

The people were reminded that this story, long ago as it was, was their own story. On the shoulders of these people they now stood. The faith of these elder fathers and mothers was their faith. They were not alone. "We are the recipients, we are the beneficiaries of the hope and faith born in that barracks. We are the great-great grandsons and granddaughters of those [who] wept and prayed that night in the place of their pain," Dr. Hicks concluded.[8] He was not simply offering a historical review. He was calling the church to act, to see their humble place, and to not think their situation novel or removed from what had gone before.

This is Malachi's message to all of God's people in all times. We can't control the stories. They control us. This is all the more evident when the story is God's. "Have we not all one Father? Did not one God create us?" asks Malachi.[9] We can fight it or embrace it. We can deny it or live in it. We can step into the wild and mysterious narrative, or we can continue the useless attempts to write our own accounts.

The choice is ours, but life — true life — beckons from the wild.

CHAPTER 4

risk of doubt

There lives more faith in honest doubt,
Believe me, than in half the creeds.

—ALFRED, LORD TENNYSON

Surely in vain have I kept my heart pure;
in vain have I washed my hands in innocence.
All day long I have been plagued;
I have been punished every morning.
If I had said, "I will speak thus,"
I would have betrayed your children.
When I tried to understand all this,
it was oppressive to me.

—PSALM 73:13-16

"Test me in this," says the LORD Almighty, "and see if I will not throw open the floodgates of heaven and pour out so much blessing that you will not have room enough for it."

—MALACHI 3:10

pastor really ought to believe in God. It works better that way. Throughout my childhood, I easily met the simple expectation that I would live and proclaim a sure confidence in the reality of God. It was never an issue. I had heard there were people who wrestled with believing in God, but I'd never actually met one. My earliest memories are of a life formed in the steady assurance of a good and readily accessible God. He was a member of the family, joining in on our conversations, settled into our routines.

You have to understand my unique upbringing to appreciate what I'm saying. My dad was an itinerant preacher until I was in the sixth grade. We owned a forty-foot trailer, and week after week, we would pack up our nomadic gooseneck home, hook it on to the back of our diesel Ford, and motor on to the next city, the next church.

It was quite a life. By the time I was twelve, I had seen most of the United States. I had explored the California badlands, wondering if we would ever see civilization again. I had experienced the Old World of Colonial Williamsburg, sat like an ant at the base of a giant sequoia, crossed the Rio Grande into the frenzied and euphoric Mexican border markets, felt the strange claustrophobic expanse of the Big Apple, and, best of all, met up with Mickey at his magical wonderland on both coasts. Few twelve-year-olds had experienced as much of the world as I had.

But even fewer twelve-year-olds were as immersed in the life of the church as I was. Throughout most of the year, my dad preached in week-long meetings, which meant we were at the church Monday through Friday and twice on Sundays. Six days a week. Forty-five weeks a year. That's a lot of church.

There was a rhythm, a routine to our life. And in the midst of that routine, significant moments stood out like a swear word in a sermon. I remember the precise day of the week when I first recognized my need for grace. It was a Friday, and I was four years old. I remember because I was wearing cowboy boots, a black western gunslinger-style vest, and a cowboy hat John Wayne would have given an approving nod. It was my favorite night of the week — western night — when all the churchgoers were encouraged to bring a friend and dress up in their best desperado attire. This wasn't very novel in New Mexico, but it was quite the affair whenever we happened to be setting up shop in Ohio.

For some reason that I can't recall, the reality of death had been on my mind, and I asked my mom what would happen to my grandma and grandpa when they died. My mom took a break from chopping vegetables for dinner and told me all about heaven. It wasn't the first time I had heard of heaven, but this time it somehow seemed more real. Death's distance had shrunk. It had nudged up closer, and my four-year-old mind noticed for the first time that eternal realities aren't just for adults. Together we went and grabbed my dad, and a little four-year-old cowboy embraced grace. It was simple. God was true. Sin was real. I needed a Savior.

After this encounter, the routine settled back in, a routine centered on doing God's work and obeying his will. We talked to God regularly, and we expected him to answer. It wasn't just that the reality of God was assumed; it was more. God defined who we were and what we did. If there were no God, there would be no us.

This pattern continued through junior high, high school, college, and into seminary. There were times when odd, pesky questions would surface. They would gnaw at me until every once in a while, usually at the most inopportune times, they would pop out. I was pretty good at shoving them back down, but not always. These debilitating questions freaked me out. I wasn't supposed to be thinking such things.

I remember one day in college when I was in the library studying. I had grabbed a book dealing with biblical authority, and I remember the heaviness that vigorously lumbered in and sat on me like a grade school bully demanding my lunch money — or else. *What if it isn't true? What if the Bible really is just like any other book?* It wouldn't let up. It just sat there, grinning, chuckling, and giving me a good slap every few seconds to remind me who was in charge.

Similar experiences happened over the years, and they made me feel weak. I wondered why I couldn't just snap out of it, couldn't just quote a Bible verse and be done with it. It unnerved me. My entire life had been lived with God's Word as the context, the foundation, the presupposition. Both in college and seminary, I studied theology. For eight years, I had been immersed in the language of faith. I was a defender of Scripture and sought to live by its claims.

My calling to pastoral ministry, my worldview, my hopes for my family, even the love I shared with my wife were all driven by one thing: God's reality. I wanted to figure out a way to just make the doubts dissipate. But I couldn't. So instead, I ignored them until they went away and I was back to the life I was used to where God was soaked into the climate.

You can imagine the terror I felt when one day the darkest question of my life surfaced. It sunk into my heart and held on like a ravenous rattler that had dug its fangs deep into a raw piece of flesh.

Is God real?

For the longest time, I couldn't voice the words. They were too abrasive, too insidious. I hoped they would just go away. I hoped if I ignored them long enough, they would forget about me. But they didn't forget. They roamed around in my head, slowly devouring more and more space until one day I was faced with what seemed an impossible reality. There was no way this could be happening to me. There was absolutely no way I could have such sinister thoughts. I didn't know for sure if I believed in God anymore.

I had become a doubter.

I was once in Yosemite in the spring. The snow from above the timberline was beginning to thaw, and the water cascaded down the mountain falls, swelling the springs and pools with frigid water, cold with a bite. The air was merely nippy, but the water was so frosty it made you gasp.

You'd think I would have known better, but one of the college buddies I was with had a moment of insanity and suggested he and I should go for a swim. Word spread that two idiots were considering taking a plunge into one of the pools, and a crowd quickly gathered. Why are humans so fascinated by watching ignorance in action, especially if it involves the possibility of pain being inflicted or people making complete fools of themselves?

Sensing we might not take the dive and they would miss the opportunity to gawk with voyeuristic thrill, the crowd began to egg us on. As the crowd grew, they goaded us even more. So we stripped down and dove in.

I can't explain the rush of adrenaline and chaos that hit me the moment the top of my head pierced the water. Every sense was immediately on edge. The roar in my head was deafening, and I felt like one of those magicians who lies on a bed of nails — except I was definitely feeling the pain slice into my skin, while the magicians never seem to wince.

When I came out of the water, everything had changed. The colors were starker. The people's faces looked unchanged, but their expressions didn't seem to mean the same things. Sound was altered. I might have heard the crunch of a small twig yards away, but I had difficulty hearing my friend — one of the smart ones — standing right next to me. "Man, that was crazy. Was it cold?"

Nothing had changed, and everything had changed.

This was exactly how I felt the moment I stared down my jolting reality. I wasn't sure of God anymore. I looked the same — same color hair, same quirky personality, same dislike for anything made with zucchini. But everything, absolutely everything, had changed.

The oddest thing is that I can't tell you why it happened. There was no trigger I could point to, no external crisis serving as the culprit. It made me feel so weak, so foolish, so alone. How could I doubt God? I had lived my whole life centered on him. Could my faith possibly be so weak as to waver without so much as a death or a disease to cause it?

I felt foolish because it seemed so in sync with suburban Americana. Compared to world standards and the realities that most Christ-followers throughout history have faced, my middle-class life didn't seem to merit a faith crisis. Many of God's people have faced torture chambers, genocide, and severe political and economic hardship. Meanwhile, I was indulging in a peculiar form of luxury by wallowing in existential confusion.

Mostly, I felt alone. Who would hear my confession of the darkness slithering across my heart? Everyone was depending on me. I was a spokesperson for God, and that meant I had to be unwavering, unflinching. I had to ignore the hollow echoes in the caverns of my soul. Dismiss the voices. Cast out the doubt. Have faith, or at least not tell anyone if I didn't.

I didn't know what to do. I was paralyzed.

I would read my Bible, a little. I would pray, a little less. But something inside me was dying, if it wasn't already dead. I would grab books proclaiming the "certainty of the faith" and desperately listen to Christian apologists who seemed to have it all together, have an answer for everything.

But there was always another question, always another doubt. Well-meaning friends would suggest I "cling to God" or "just reject the doubts." Sounds reasonable, but if it were all an elaborate façade, a hoax, I would be holding on to a lie. The emperor might have believed he wore the finest silks and woolen blends, but that didn't make it so.

The doubts were debilitating. They gripped my heart and squeezed the very life out of me. I didn't know who I was anymore, a stranger in my own body. Thankfully, the confusion would ease off a bit every now and then, allowing me to function. But I was never totally free. It was as if there was this constant presence, a shadowy possibility of something dreadful hovering over my shoulder.

The worst was when it stole from me the pleasure of praying over my sons. Bedtime is a beautiful time with our boys. Because Wyatt is older, there is more to his regimen. Most nights we do a bath with a yellow ducky, a spongy turtle, a quartet of rubber frogs, and finger paints. We play, we splash, and sometimes we sing.

After the bath, we attempt to get Wyatt to brush his teeth, but usually he ends up swallowing the toothpaste and using the wet bristles to brush other places, such as his hair or in between his toes.

Next, we give him a fresh diaper and pull on his pj's. My favorite is the green and blue pair with the big *G* embroidered across the chest (if you can guess where they were purchased, you are proof of the far reaches of the marketing power of corporate America). Then he starts the chant, "Book, book, book." He rumbles through his bookshelf, deciding on one for that night's story time. I like the story about a guy named Bob who likes to build.

Then Wyatt tosses the book onto his bed, and I toss Wyatt onto his bed. I dive in myself and read him the story. When we finish, he claps his hands together and says, "Gin, gin" (he is asking me to read it *again*, not for an adult nightcap). Some nights I indulge him; some nights I don't.

When we are done and it is time for him to go "night-night," I turn off his light and flip on his noise maker, filling the room with gentle, cascading sounds perfect for a long night's rest. Then I go back over to his bed and pick him up as he clutches his "night-night" blanket. He lays his head on my shoulder and wraps his arms around my neck. I ask him if he wants me to pray to Jesus, and he enthusiastically pleads, "Peese, peese."

It's truly beautiful.

But one night, the beauty was ripped away from me. The prayer I spoke was filled with familiar words: "God, watch over him. Whisper to him, even now, that you are his God."

Yet silently, the lurking shadows welled up. From the darkest corner of my mind, the doubts lurched forward. *What if it isn't true? What if you are praying to nothing but empty space? Do you believe it?*

Fear gripped me. I held my son in steady arms, but I was trembling. *What if . . . ?*

It's a hideous place to be. Unsure, entirely unsettled, I didn't know what to do with myself. I hated it. Damn the doubts. I just wanted to go back, to rewind to the time when things were simpler, easier, and the answers were always certain. I pleaded for God to take the doubts away.

I believed doubts were the enemy that had to be slain so faith could emerge. I supposed that I only needed to muster up more of my reasoning skills and more determination. With them as my allies, certainly I could put doubt to its final rest and thus resurrect faith.

I have come to believe I was, at least in part, wrong. The more I have explored the biblical theme of faith, the more complex and surprising I have found it to be. Faith has more grit than I had thought. It blossoms in the most unexpected places. It is nurtured in hostile climates and takes root in uninhabitable soil. Like fresh evergreen sprouts rising from the ashes of the scorched forest, faith burgeons where it wants, when it wants.

Faith makes its own way. It is not timid. For so long I saw faith as a hesitant energy, needing to be gently coddled and then coaxed to peek out and show itself. I thought faith needed my help, and it was my place to defend it against any assailant. I had to suck it up, silence the doubts, and make certain faith was offered an inviting environment where it could germinate.

I had a weak view of faith. Faith is sturdy. It can handle its own battles. This hearty warrior does not shy away from doubts. In some ways, it seems to revel in them. True faith—honest, gut-wrenching, turn-your-knuckles-white-while-you-hang-on-for-dear-life faith — appears to be a close cousin to doubt.

My effort was aimed at figuring out my doubts, deciphering them, dismantling them, and quelling them — finally, completely. I have come to believe that my effort was severely misguided. My problem is not so much with doubts. My problem is with faith. For me, faith has often equaled some form of unflinching assurance. To have faith is to *know*, and to know, in my sense, is to have siphoned away every uncertainty. Faith, essentially, is the absence of mystery.

As I now see it, faith and doubt are bedfellows — strange ones, indeed, but partners all the same. Faith requires, to at least some degree, some possibility that I could be wrong.

This is not to say that doubt can never be evil. Doubt that is nurtured as a foundational distrust for God and never submits to the authority of biblical revelation demonstrates a heart unwilling to yield to divine truth. This is sin. However, wrestling and struggling with God's revelation and how it conflicts with our fallen world is, I am suggesting, part of what it means to be human, created with the faculty to think and question and wonder.[1]

This earthy view of faith allows me to echo the sentiments of Avery Cardinal Dulles: "Faith . . . is not a simple achievement of reason. It is the work of reason submitting to the word of God, which comes by way of revelation. God, as the infinite source of all that is or can be, lies immeasurably beyond all that we can infer from the created order."[2] And because of this reality — the tension between the God who is revealed and the God who is beyond — faith by necessity ventures into a realm that is something other than certifiable surety.

Faith is a risk, a gamble. When Christ called his followers, he often spoke in a language daring them to wager. They were asked to leave behind family, professions, reputations, and positions of social power.

In return, they were offered a wandering life in which they would often be without a bed and rarely would know where their next meal would come from. They would be powerless and penniless, and though they seemed to miss the clues, they were forewarned that the One who called them to this insane existence would die a brutal criminal's death.

Christ asked them to roll the dice, to throw all their chips on red and let it ride. On a promise. On One who called himself God. On eternity. On something they couldn't see.

Faith always makes such requests. Faith is leaping when you can't see what is below. Faith is offering a kiss before you are certain it will be returned. Faith believes that what we see in dim reflections and hear in subtle whispers is truer than what sits three feet in front of us.

Faith owns up to the terror of not knowing, and at the same time, it causes us to marvel at the paradoxical reality that there is nothing in the world we could be more sure of. Pascal knew this well when he lamented, "Seeing too much to deny, and too little to be sure, I am in a state to be pitied."[3] This is the crucible of faith: Absolute certainty eludes me, yet I am compelled to believe. It is all I have. It is my only hope.

I would expect God to grow perturbed with me when I am mired in these mucky places of doubt, when I just don't know and yet fall forward because it is all I have. My view of God is too developed to expect severe anger. I don't envision a heaven-sized lashing or lightning strikes hurled with precision in my direction. But annoyance seems in order. I imagine God's frustration with me, wondering how I could be so childish to think that following him could ever be sized up as risky.

However, Malachi offers a different view of God's take on faith, doubt, and the notion of risk. Rather than dismissing our moments of indecision as roadblocks to faith, God at times seems to expect them, capitalize on them, even invite them.

God's people faced economic hardship. Political realities and natural forces combined to put them under a strain. The taxes levied by the Persian Empire were moderately heavy, and they apparently faced a drought that made their agricultural livelihood sparse. For a people whose history was riddled with oppression from foreign powers and long seasons of battling with the elements in order to survive in their desert climate, their state of affairs was not unanticipated. It was just hard. But they would make it. They would spend a little less, save a little more. Frugality would save the day.

God, however, didn't think much of their frugalness. He wanted them to dare a little, to step out on the edge, peer over, and jump off. Israel's spiritual malaise and frugal tendencies had tempted them to go the other direction, to hoard and tighten their fists. As they did, they stopped bringing their offerings to the temple. When they did come to worship, they didn't bring all God had required. They skimped and kept more for themselves. I can understand their predicament. They were in a difficult place. *Certainly God will understand*, they must have thought.

God understood far more than they could have imagined. God understood that their tightened purse strings reflected a constricted heart. God understood that their ability to believe, their ability to have faith at all, was at stake. The people's insistence on being safe, warm, secure, and snuggly would, in the end, keep them from embracing him.

If God is daring and bold and free, if God skirts the wild edges, then following him means we will make friends with hazard and peril. As we grow into our calling as his people and experience more resonance with his heart, we will be discontent to remain nestled in the comforting fireside glow, where danger never nips at our heels and impending peril never sends stabs of panic through our heart.

So God asked the people to risk. While they were under the burden of taxes and wrestling with the soil for food, God asked them for their cash and their crops — the full portion. He asked them to leap.

His exact words were, "Test me." It's a gambling phrase, and God asked his people to step up to the slot machine, drop in their coins, and pull the lever.[4] See what will happen, he said. Gamble on me. Risk.

But faith as certainty — the kind of faith I embraced before my tumble into doubts — has no concept of this sense of danger and daring. Faith grounded in complete, verifiable proof leaves no room (or need) for risk. This pseudofaith works against doubt, whereas God-styled faith works with it.

A lesser view of faith wants to protect God, to shield him against hard questions or unsavory press. God doesn't share the concern. Confident in his own reality, he doesn't fret over humanity's God-dilemma of whether to believe or not.

Philip Yancey has said that God seems to say, "Here I am. Here is the truth. Do with it as you will." God isn't scared off by our doubts. If Malachi is any indication, he might even expect them. Might it be that God's claims are so outlandish, so otherworldly, so God-sized that respecting them properly and taking them seriously demands some degree of risk and thus some degree of doubt?

Could it be that on some level, doubt indicates we have heard God correctly and we tremble? God is quite self-assured, and our doubt is no crisis for him. Our doubt might even point to reality, merely demonstrating that he is God and we are not. It is as if he knows that in the end, we will abandon ourselves to him, doubt and faith all mixed together. Where else could we go? To whom else could we turn?

In moments when the darkness lurks, I often spiral back into the despairing questions. I hate it. It is painful. In the end, rarely do I have more answers than when I began the gloomy dive.

But I always come back to the same place. *A pastor really ought to believe in God. It works better that way.* I can't help but believe. I can't *not* believe. It isn't entirely rational. It's far from mathematical precision. But it's where my heart ends up resting. When you have your dark night of the soul, you will have to find your own conclusion, but for me, it comes down to a simple matter of options. And I don't have any others.

Where else would I go? Who else has stirred me more? What other reality has offered me more beauty, more rest, more sense of self? And so I return to God. I sit back down. In this returning, I see doubt as faith's friend. Doubt does what any true friend will: It keeps us honest. And this process of questioning, Tennyson reminds us, makes certain our faith is honest. Doubt strains our ideals and sifts through all we say we believe. In this painful process, doubt is the sledgehammer that shatters what will not stand up to its ferocious assault. However, if truth is what we want — and if God is true as he declares himself to be — then after we emerge from the dark night, what we have is more of God, more of what is real. Such destruction is apparently required. Falsehoods must be ripped away so truth can stand, bold and clear.

Saint John of the Cross believed that for the human soul's Godward journey, more crucial than discovering what God *is* is to discover what God *is not*. The gloomy corridors of doubt are one means of saving us from our erroneous perceptions of God, of pulling us from what God is not.

Recently when Miska had her own bout with doubt, she said, "You know, I keep thinking of Peter's words to Christ when he asked the disciples if they too would abandon him. They answered, 'Where else would we go? Only you have the words of life.'"[5]

Amen, Peter. Where else would I go?

Before Mel Gibson's controversial film, *The Passion of the Christ*, hit the big screen, Diane Sawyer sat down with him on *ABC News' Primetime Live* for a frank interview. Everyone wanted him to respond to the accusations of anti-Semitism and historical inaccuracy.

However, the most poignant portions of the interview came when the conversation turned personal. There were raw moments when Gibson was emotionally exposed and offered how deeply he had been affected by the story of Christ.

At one point, Gibson said, "I have to believe."

"You have to believe?" asked a confused Diane Sawyer.

"I have to. . . ."

"Why?"

Gibson responded with an intense reply: "So I can hope. So I can live."[6]

This is faith. Staring doubt down. Refusing to pretend it doesn't exist. And hoping, even against the odds at times, that in the end faith will win the day.

Tonight a bit of the beauty returned. The boys got their bath. We played with them, read them a story, and turned out their lights. When I leaned over to give each of them their final kiss good night, I offered the usual ritual. I placed my thumb on their heads and rubbed it in the shape of a cross. As I imprinted them with this invisible symbol of all I believe in faith, I spoke holy words: "Bless you, my son."

CHAPTER 5

twilight knowing

If you restrict knowledge to that which you can put into words, your model of knowledge doesn't offer any help concerning how to get off the starting block or out of the gate.

— ESTHER LIGHTCAP MEEK

The sacraments do not merely make the word visible; they make it tasty, aromatic, tactile. They appeal to all the senses.

— LEONARD J. VANDER ZEE

"Israel, I, the LORD, have loved you. And yet you ask in what way have I loved you."

— MALACHI 1:2, CEV

Last Thursday I began my day with an early morning stop at Wal-Mart's tire and lube center to have my Honda Accord serviced. I pulled up to the maintenance bay, handed the attendant my keys, and went into the lobby. The sitting areas in auto service centers have a surprising similarity to one another. You'll always find a pot of free coffee sitting in a corner where it has settled in for a couple of days, ink-black, gooey, and smelling like burnt rubber. A small television with splotchy sound and rabbit ears is usually precariously hoisted up on a shelf or cabinet, offering viewing choices limited to *Montel Williams* or a played-out kid's movie. The room is dingy yet somehow feels sterile — an odd mix.

This sitting area was no different. The coffee greeted me with its pungent tar aroma. *Snow Dogs* was on the television, and this seemed to make the small girl sitting on the edge of her hard plastic chair very excited because she was loud. Very loud.

All was as it should be — until I looked at the magazines on the table next to me. At the top of the stack sat *Biblical Archaeology Review*. In case you haven't skimmed an issue lately, allow me to introduce you. The *Review* is not a high-circulation magazine. It probably has only a slightly larger readership than *IRS Monthly*. The *Review* highlights the latest developments in archaeological digs and is a forum for scholars to debate the nuances of Ancient Near Eastern findings and other developments in the historical study of early cultures. There are reports about the craftsmanship of clay pots and arguments over the precise dates of Mesopotamian kingdoms.

Don't misunderstand me. If archaeology or highly technical theology is your love, then the *Biblical Archaeology Review* would be of great interest to you. However, this sort of person wouldn't seem to make up a high proportion of the Wal-Mart tire and lube center's clientele. *Muscle & Fitness, Inside NASCAR, Reader's Digest*, even *O: The Oprah Magazine* — all of these periodicals would make sense. However, finding a copy of the *Biblical Archaeology Review* in the sitting area of Wal-Mart's auto service center is like finding Gandhi in attendance at an NRA convention. It doesn't fit.

I picked it up and perused its pages. One article grabbed my attention, and I began reading. It was a conversation among several biblical scholars, and some of their opinions did not fit well within a more historic, orthodox view of Christian Scripture. It was fascinating and challenging. It stretched my mind and made me evaluate my assumptions. I think it was healthy. However, the more I tussled with the material, the more my mind bogged down with confusion. I was attempting to coherently analyze conflicting evidence, opposing presuppositions, and varying interpretations of material that can be read quite differently by scholars coming to the enterprise from varying starting points.

Such endeavors are good and necessary. A Christian faith that has not been well investigated, poked at, and even, from time to time, dismantled so one can peer — really, honestly peer — at all the parts hints at a faith that might be more about denial than truth and integrity. If our faith in God is true, then it can withstand difficult reflection and disturbing questions. This is a healthy process because sometimes amid the disconcerting investigation, we find that some of our beliefs are in error. They are not God's truth as we had thought. We were mistaken, and distressing as it might be, it is good for our faith to be instructed, to have the excess stripped away.

However, such a process is not the only way to buttress our faith. It might not even be the best way. Hershel Shanks has made a career of investigating the scientific, historical, and archaeological evidence surrounding the Christian faith and the biblical witness that testifies to it. In much of his academic research, I find a theme, a nagging question he continues to ask: *How can I know? How can I be sure of the veracity of this Book that claims Divinity?*

Scientific investigation, scholarly wrangling, philosophical fine-tuning, anthropological inquiry—all of the tools of precision aimed at leveling ambiguity fail to deliver their intended result: certainty. Shanks's conclusion is that in the end, after all his tireless and mentally stimulating exertion in the historical sciences, his investigation does not answer the question of Scripture's truthfulness. He has determined that it simply can't.

"This is reflecting . . . my own search for answers that I can't find," Shanks says. "If I ever write a book on 'How True Is the Bible?' I'll have to start out by saying that archaeology is not the way to find out, that it has very little to say."[1]

In a culture nourished from its infancy in the Enlightenment, it can feel almost sacrilegious to suggest that factual verification and laboratory-style experimentation are not the only ways to arrive at knowledge, to embrace truth. To further suggest that there are some types of knowing for which these ingrained paths are less than helpful, if not entirely inadequate, is nefarious.

Some things you just know. You can't prove it. You can't explain it. You can't strip it bare and stick it on a cold, sterile steel plate to probe and prod it under a high-powered microscope. It isn't an apparatus you can break down, finger through its components, and catalog all your findings. It simply *is*.

The gnawing pit in your stomach is caused by the strange elixir called love. Krispy Kreme donuts grabbed while the neon light flashes "Hot Donuts Now" taste better than the grocery store variety available behind the greasy glass bin. A mom has a second sense, an intuition, that her child is in trouble.

Some things you just know.

Most of us are familiar, even comfortable, with this intuitive sense as long as we don't make much of it and it doesn't invade the more important arenas of our life, the areas requiring, you know, *real* knowledge. In these allegedly more substantive spheres, precise definitions, tangible data, concrete observations, pie charts, statistics, and cold, uncluttered scrutiny reign. What we can prove, what we can coolly and objectively analyze, determines what we can really know.

But there is another realm of knowing — something more than a simple intuitive sense and more than a slavish reliance on hard data . It dances in the twilight, that magically mysterious moment that refuses to be defined by the normal prescribed categories of day and night. Twilight is neither. It is both. It is somewhere in between. It is more.

This twilight place is where poets, dreamers, prophets, and lovers find themselves most at home. They know deeply, but what they know isn't limited to what they see — at least not with the eyes most are accustomed to trusting. They see things that are but aren't. They hear what is whispered between the crevices of our words. They trust there is more, even if they can't exactly explain why.

Kathleen Norris tells us that "the discipline of poetry teaches poets, at least, that they often have to say things they can't pretend to understand."[2] And in that twilight speaking, there is a knowing. A knowing that our language can't capture, our vocabulary can't describe. Yet it is there. It beats with life. God resides there; it is God's twilight.

The question demanding an answer is whether or not we will embrace this twilight place. Will we insist on mere precision and in doing so lose the nuance, the harmony, the deeper shades of grace? This is no demand to leave behind what we know or to haphazardly dismiss the familiar. This is certainly not a repudiation of the more objective ways of knowing and perceiving reality that we have grown accustomed to. It is a simple offering of more. To explore the twilight is not to dismiss the rugged beauty of the day or the quiet sanctity of the night. Without the context of these, twilight would not be.

My openness to the twilight, to ways of knowing that are more organic and less systematic, is slow in coming. I have always trusted what I can see, what I can taste, or what I can wrap my arms around. I have often taken the role of the skeptic, the cool-headed guy with a steady sense of reason and a good dose of common sense. Others — those less grounded in reality or less analytical — might get hoodwinked or snookered, but not me. I would demand rational proof, and if it wasn't provided, I would keep my distance. I'm a hard sell.

I am realizing that what I actually am is foolish. Most of our world doesn't fit into the clearly distinguishable categories of absolute, verifiable reality or entirely confirmable nonsense. It's murkier than that. Even in the hard sciences, there is a growing admission that the notion of objective, demonstrable certainty is most often a myth.

In *Biology as Ideology: The Doctrine of DNA*, R. C. Lewontin, a geneticist and Harvard professor, critiqued science's urban fable that it is a wholly objective enterprise, removed from intuition, mystery, and social experiences. Though certainly no advocate for any version of a divine worldview (as well as no antagonist toward modern science), he compares science to religion, explaining how each has a "certain mystical and veiled quality so that its innermost operation is not completely transparent to everyone."[3]

It would seem that however diligently we might try, we can't conclusively separate knowledge, whether scientific or spiritual, from some manner of faith. Michael Ruse, a scientific philosopher with an agnostic bent, has observed that many of the foundations of modern scientific theory, true as he believes them to be, are based as much in metaphysics as any other path toward knowledge.

Human experience bears out this reality. There is a certain encounter that is almost universally held to be an enjoyable, desirable act. In most societies, some form of this act is viewed with delight. This act is a kiss.

What is it about the kiss that is so attractive, so alive? If we are kissed by one who holds our hearts, why do we blush or feel our hearts quicken? If it is abused, like the Judas act, why do we view it as a despicable treachery?

This collective reality can't be ultimately explained by the laws of science or by the well-oiled process of deductive reasoning. Philosophical inquiry may offer interesting perspectives on the experience. Biological assumptions about hormone levels and the power of human kinetic activity will give added insight. Psychological theorems of our evolved emotive responses will give us food for thought. However, in the end, all of these will leave us cold, chilled by the hygienic efforts to reduce something so innately human, so raw, to principles and proof. We know something is missing.

A kiss can't be fully explained by analyzing its individual components. A kiss is not attractive because it is some inevitable, long-proven human reaction to the contact of our lips with the prescribed elements of heat and moisture. If that were the case, we could get the same response from contact with a warm towel.

We experience — we know — that a kiss is pleasurable, desirable, and good because there is something deeply intuitive in us, something that can't be captured with description and explained with the precision of mathematics or the exactitude of cerebral analysis.

As I am typing this, I am listening to Christopher Parkening's melodiously rich *Courante from Cello Suite 3*. It is light yet thoughtful. It draws me in with its simple tones and subtle vigor. One's musical preference might not gravitate to the classical guitar, but I am willing to venture that virtually anyone, regardless of age or culture or worldview, would find this piece beautiful. Even if the style, tempo, or genre isn't what one prefers, there is something exquisite in these chords that transcends objections. Beauty goes deeper.

I don't know that I can get at what it is exactly, which actually supports the point. But this sort of beauty has substance, and it resonates with life. It is a whisper, a hum we can't ignore. It is like when Miska blows gently on my ear, persistently, softly, perhaps to wake me up or get my attention when I am deep in distraction. I might not comprehend what is happening immediately, but it can't be disregarded or denied for long. It is there, and its presence brushes against me until I take note. Beauty in music, art, and Scripture blows gently until we pay attention.

Esther Lightcap Meek proposes that "what the modern model of knowledge refused to admit was the existence and necessity of knowing that can't be put into words. And in so doing, it missed the lived feel of the thing."[4]

As a young adult, Philip Yancey left the church, disillusioned and wary. Multiple friendships and experiences played their part in wooing him back to the faith, but he says that it was the "beauty of nature, classical music, and romantic love" that compelled him to embrace God anew.[5] This is not everyone's experience, but for some, perhaps many, it is the existential, ethereal truths that end up being the most convincing suggestions of God's movement in the world.

C. S. Lewis asks how we can explain pleasure apart from God. This is a profound question. How can I make sense of the invigorating hope I have that my boys will live in ways that offer vibrant meaning to their world? Aside from acknowledging a Creator who has woven a sense of ecstasy into my soul, how can I explain the passions I feel for my wife, the joy I receive in capturing a brief glance of her dancing eyes or hearing her spontaneous, free laugh? Why do the midnight New Mexico skies, erupting with the brilliance of stars on fire, speak so loudly to me, communicating something I can't explain yet can't deny?

It must be that there are words spoken in a language more of the heart than of the mind. There must be ways of perceiving, ways of knowing, that are more intuitive, more organic, more primitive than the tightly reasoned paths I usually tread.

The poet is versed in such language. It is her dialect. Poetry is sensual, inviting us to step in and experience rather than to dissect and diagram. Poetry is something we feel, something that gets down inside us and rummages around. The poet can't be deciphered. She must simply be listened to, taken in, and embraced. There are many realities that ask to be known in the same way.

I am coming to these conclusions with baby steps. It is hard for me to acknowledge there are ways of seeing the world that do not conform to my ability to verify. Some of my struggles with faith and my inability to feel God's presence seem to stem from my insistence that God make himself known to me in ways I am comfortable with, in ways I can control.

God is refusing me. He is hemming me in, just as he told Israel's prophets he would do to those he loved.[6] Malachi's message is one of hemming in, of standing in the way. The center thrust of Malachi's words is this: God is not subservient to our whims. He can be known. He can be experienced. It is his heart to give himself away. However, it will be on his terms, not ours.

My demand for control rises out of fear. I feel it rise up within me when my grip on my world, my surroundings, or my relationships seems in peril. Like a wolf tenaciously protecting its last winter kill, something inside me clinches up and bears its teeth when threatened. One way I maintain control is by eliminating uncertainty, by planning my surroundings or arranging my footing so that I have well-reasoned and unassailable assurance. The rational world where concrete facts hold sway is my comfort zone. I am able to minimize risk. I am able to stay in control. I like guarantees, sure things. I like it when I can point to clear reasons why something is so. I like it when I can say that any reasonable person looking objectively at the same facts should come to the same conclusion. It makes me feel safe. I am in control. I have no reason to fear.

But when these avenues are blocked and this kind of moral certainty is refused me, then it all breaks down. Something inside turns frantic. I am afraid.

But what exactly *am I afraid of?*

A friend recently posed this very question to me: "Winn, what are you afraid of?" Point-blank, it stared me in the face. And it didn't blink. Why is control so important to me? Why does the ambiguous or unforeseeable terrify me? In some ways, I am a risk taker. I like to challenge the status quo. In certain environments, I am daring. So why in deep matters of the soul is everything within me bent on maintaining equilibrium? Why does the fear of tilting off the high wire cause me to shrivel inside?

I don't know all the answers. I am fairly certain I still have a good bit of work to do in learning more of the questions. However, the more I converse with Malachi, the more I see that I am in the same predicament as those who first heard God's fiery words. I am committed to using God to make me safe, to bring order out of my chaos. God is not God to me. He is a tool, a means to an end.

When God is not God to me, I continue to believe the perverse lie that making my world right and holding things together is *my* job. That is quite a task, and to make it work, I fling every ounce of effort and arrange every resource at my disposal toward this end. In this environment, there is no place for ambiguity. There is no place for something that falls outside the bounds of mathematical probability. I have worked the numbers and collected the data. I know what needs to be done to preserve what I believe must be maintained.

Being God is a big job, and when I grab the role, there is a lot at stake. The first hint of equivocation or the first suggestion that something might not play along as it is supposed to incites an insurgence. All my energy, my entire arsenal, is directed at squelching the insurrection. I have to maintain control. It is the only way to keep things from running off the rail and getting completely out of hand.

During the last few weeks, I've noticed my frustration level rising with my older son, Wyatt. He is two. Need I say more? He is erratic and demanding. He is loud — very loud. And he is more than a tad bit sneaky. If you leave him alone for even a few minutes, he will invariably commit one of a short list of preschool crimes: He might craftily pilfer the "secret" candy stash (located seven feet off the ground, I might add), or he might make a quiet, mad dash out the front door in a manner that would make any convict proud.

He is a handful, but he is two. It's to be expected. Yet lately, I've grown unhealthily impatient. I've been sterner than necessary and less playful than I would desire. I experience frustration because I feel as if I am losing control. I want to see Wyatt grow up to be a well-adjusted adult. I want him to respect authority and succeed in life. And somehow, these two-year-old antics put that in jeopardy. Wyatt isn't fitting into my prescribed plan for how he should develop, and he isn't responding to all the discipline tricks I thought were sure bets. Wyatt doesn't want to play by my rules.

So I bear down. I dissect every interaction and come up with new tricks. I want to up the ante and douse the danger that Wyatt might not turn out exactly as I have planned.

I know each child is unique, and I've heard all about the need to nurture a child's heart rather than force him or her into a mold. But you have to understand, my plan is on the line — and I can't figure out how to make Wyatt fit in. I want a formula. I want proof. I want to know how to raise him the way a farmer knows how to handle his crops. Plant this month. Harvest that month. It's all by the book. It's certain and well established. We know — the *Farmers' Almanac* says so.

Little of my life follows the routine. My life as a dad, a husband, a friend didn't come with an almanac. I have to feel my way, to yield to mystery, to trust, to listen to the Spirit.

As I have repented of my arrogance in thinking I can control my son and manage his development, I have felt a fresh freedom. It has been a freedom to allow Wyatt to simply be Wyatt, convictlike dashes for the front yard included. It has been a freedom to allow my own hopes to be merely that — hopes rather than demands.

Trusting what is outside the range of my control is dangerous. It opens me up to the possibility that I will fail or that I might have my hopes utterly crushed. Those parts of my personality that might be described as risky — trying new ventures or challenging the accepted modes of operation or patterns of thinking — might at times surface as expressions of my long-tested *modus operandi*. A certain amount of adrenaline and a certain amount of overturning the apple cart is part of the equation, one of the elements that makes my world tick. So even living daringly can be a means to maintaining balance.

The kind of risk God calls me to — surrendering to him as sovereign God, outside my parameters, almost dismissive of my boundaries — is a risk I want to hold at bay. Yet most of what we are able to know in our lives involves risk and some element of trust. We just rarely notice it because there is little consequence if it goes poorly. The kinds of foods we enjoy, the comedies we laugh at (or groan at), the way we enjoy being touched, the colors we like to wear — these are all deeply profound truths. These things we know come much closer to the center of who we are than historic facts or political convictions ever will.

With these simple "knowings," we trust intuition. We trust our senses and our experiences. No one can convince me that I am mistaken and in fact really *do* like brussels sprouts. They can protest all they like. I know. Yet there is risk involved. Someday, I might wake up and find brussels sprouts to be less disgusting, tasty even. Perhaps my taste buds will change. Perhaps they will be fried and, like everything else that is battered and dunked in hot grease, taste like chicken. There is much that is uncertain about the future. Yet I take a risk. In my gut, I know the truth, and I run with it.

Much of our knowledge comes in such a way. It takes a commitment, a certain trusting. Meek acknowledges this assumption: "The act of knowing is a risky disposing of our beings, a passionate commitment to trust things we cannot fully justify at the time of our effort. Just as the person who truly lays out for a Frisbee risks crashing to the ground, with or without the Frisbee."[7]

Meek makes an important clarification, however, that this is not irrational risk. This kind of knowledge is not contrary to facts. It is not blind faith. It does not work against logic, even if it can't always be deduced by it. This kind of knowledge is not making your own truth, nor is it affirming the silly notion that there is no such thing as a universal reality. This risk-taking, twilight-knowing way of understanding is simply giving sway to realism. It is an expression of what God calls faith, of seeing what is unseen by the usual, normal ways of seeing.

The unborn child speaking in the final stanzas of the poem "Wean Yourself" by Rumi rebuffed such ways of seeing, such faith:

> *Think how it is to have a conversation with an embryo.*
> *You might say, "The world outside is vast and intricate.*
> *There are wheatfields and mountain passes,*
> *and orchards in bloom.*
>
> *At night there are millions of galaxies, and in sunlight*
> *the beauty of friends dancing at a wedding."*
>
> *You ask the embryo why he, or she, stays cooped up*
> *in the dark with eyes closed.*
> *Listen to the answer.*

There is no "other world."
I only know what I've experienced.
You must be hallucinating.[8]

It is not that seeing with our eyes, touching with our hands, or figuring out with our minds is unnecessary. On the contrary, a world without these realities would yield chaos. However, there are moments, times, and places when we have to embrace other voices and more subtle ways of experiencing. Sometimes truth can seem like a hallucination.

This is the beauty of the sacraments Christ offers his church. They are a way of experiencing God, of embracing him. Much of the church has long spoken of the dual, intricately blended ways of encountering God and stirring up faith: Word and sacraments. The Word might be described as what God has spoken, what he has said for us to hear and obey. The sacraments might be described as how God touches, what he provides as a means for allowing our senses to brush against him, to get the sense of him, to savor him.

Some of the fiercest theological battles have been fought over attempts to capture the precise nuances of these physical encounters with faith. I wonder if at least some of these bloodbaths have more to do with our addiction to precision and our aversion to mystery than they do to unpolluted doctrinal commitment. If we don't understand it, we will beat the life out of it until we do.[9]

My sense is that Jesus holds little concern for long treatises defining his rather simple words, "This is my body. This is my blood." Lounging around the table enhanced by the aroma of fresh bread, freshly ripened olives, and fruits bursting with flavor, he inaugurated a meal, a gathering of God's people around the table. The invitation is to savor, to salivate, to chew, to feel. It isn't something we can too rigidly demarcate. Like twilight, it is another way of knowing, another way of experiencing.

At times, arguments fall short and thoughtful perspicuity fails to deliver the hope of final, authoritative certainty. We need something more. We need to touch and be touched. We need to have our hearts warmed. We need to hear a word spoken by a means that is able to articulate what we have been unable to enunciate on our own. We need to know, but in a way that feels strangely unlike all the other ways we have known. These other ways are good, but in this instance, they just won't do.

Vander Zee echoes this sentiment: "The blessing of sacramental worship is the thrill and comfort of knowing that God meets us where we are, washing us, feeding us, quenching our thirst for grace. We not only believe it, we sense it, see it, taste it, feel it, smell it and swallow it. What my mind doubts, my mouth tastes as the Lord's goodness. When my faith falters, my fingers can touch the truth."[10]

On some Sundays when I doubt, I need to hear God's verbal words proclaimed. On other Sundays when my faith falters, my mouth needs to taste God's goodness. I need to actually *touch* the truth.

John Calvin knew as much. When cornered to give ultimate theological clarity to God's mysterious ways of interacting with his people in the sacraments, he resisted. "I will not be ashamed," he declared, "to confess that it is too high a mystery either for my mind to comprehend or my words to express; and to speak more plainly, *I rather feel than understand it.*"[11] Much as the idol of rationalism fights against it, there are times when knowing means *feeling* as much as (and on a few occasions, even more than) *understanding*.

Peter Hiett, my former pastor, says, "Maybe faith isn't the correct answer to a problem as much as accepting a great invitation to dance."[12] Dancing, music, laughter, kisses, passion, desire — these belong to the twilight. And our God is a romancing God, a God of melodies and fire and ardor. To dance with him is to step into the twilight.

Lately, as I've surrendered my demands for a surefire technique for raising my sons, I have felt a deep stirring, a delight in my boys. We have played like madmen. We have run and jumped and tickled and raced plastic trucks and taken spontaneous trips to get ice cream. I have felt fresh life. I have stepped into the twilight.

CHAPTER 6

sex and sacrament

Only when we perceive that these poor bodies are the natural (as opposed to supernatural) expression of God's glory, so that nakedness is as close as most of us will ever get to seeing God in the flesh, only then can we begin to understand that sex is the closest thing (next to the Eucharist) to touching Him.

—MIKE MASON

The absolute yearning of one human body for another particular one . . . is one of life's major mysteries.

—IRIS MURDOCH

Has not the LORD made them one? In flesh and spirit they are his.

—MALACHI 2:15

hen Miska first told me she wanted a morning wedding (10:30 a.m. to be exact), I was a little surprised. I had never heard of anyone getting married in the morning. I wondered if it were even allowed. As planning progressed, I found out this was only the tip of the iceberg of what I didn't know about weddings.

As she explained it, however, it was obvious that Miska's reasoning for the time of our ceremony was inspired. Virtually all the pictures would be taken before the wedding. We would enjoy our service and the exchanging of our vows. We would celebrate with friends and family at the reception. We would shove cake in each other's mouths, being sure to spread a bit of the icing on one another's nose.

And then we would be done and on our honeymoon — all before 2:00 p.m.

Suddenly it made perfect sense. Why would anyone get married at any other time?

We added one scandalous wrinkle to the plans. During the preceremony photography session, Miska and I had our pictures as a couple taken. Protests were lodged that we would attract the bad luck believed to descend when a groom sees his bride in her dress before the walk down the aisle, but we did it anyway.

The photographer snapped several rolls of film, and after he finished, we asked for a few minutes alone. The large sanctuary of the church was empty, and the grand oak doors were closed. There I stood with my soon-to-be wife. She wore the most unbelievable dress. Pure white, it flowed gracefully yet was snug in all the proper places. Her long, dark hair was pulled up, beautifully displaying her tanned neck. Her eyes were deep, alive. She was positively stunning, and I was captured by her beauty.

There was something transcendent about that moment — the large, sacred space, the stillness of the room, the gravity of what we were about to embark upon, the sheer magnificence of this woman standing before me, holding my hands and probing deeply into my eyes. In that moment, every sense I possessed piqued with intense desire. It was raw. Enflamed. Holy.

In ways I cannot explain, I sensed that in the moments to follow, I would be crossing a threshold, a gateway into a deeper spiritual realm. I would be making promises that placed me into an ancient story, a very ancient design. In the hours that followed, I would be physically joined to my love, the one who would soon be called my wife. And in this joining, another chapter of this story begun before time would be penned. What we were stepping into — with the vows and the expressions of bodily oneness — was no mere civil union. Our act was not just a sensible, private decision to share our individual resources out of mutual commitment (or even affection). We were characters in God's drama, living symbols of divine truth. We were diving into a script we were not writing and could not control, something Paul reminds us is a mystery.[1]

This is not to say our wedding day was entirely otherworldly. It was joyous and exhilarating and tiring, and it even had its unplanned and undesirable moments, a few of which are still embarrassing for me. There is the unfortunate fact that anyone who sees the groom pictures taken before the service will notice I had put my wedding ring on the wrong hand. Then there is the evidence, forever preserved on video, of my jittery nerves during the ceremony. In strenuously tense moments, I have the awkward tendency to laugh. I fought back laughter while the pastor gave the wedding charge. I sporadically chuckled during the vows. My muffled giggles made my shoulders shake during the solemn time of prayer and the lighting of the unity candle. Miska was more than a little incredulous.

If anyone somehow missed either of these misfortunes, they had only to follow us a few miles on our departure from the reception to observe another mishap. A friend had loaned us a Mercedes convertible. It was our chance to leave the scene in style. However, the temperature was in the high nineties that day, and the Arkansas humidity was hovering in the same range. It was sweltering. Having already accomplished the grand, romantic exit from the wedding site, we were no longer enamored with the luxury of a convertible, exposed to the sun and heat. Also, we were going to have to hit the freeway, and Miska hadn't planned to have her hair and wedding dress whip through the wind as we cruised past the afternoon traffic. It just didn't fit in with the fairytale feel of the day.

Ever the caring and considerate groom, I pulled over to close the top. I pushed every button and yanked every switch, but I couldn't get it to work. So we lumbered down the interstate, sweat gushing and Miska wrestling with her dream of a dress as those in passing cars gawked at the couple who were "Just Married" and obviously had no clue that it didn't make sense to ride with the top down. What did we care? We were heading toward our honeymoon.

After our first night in the honeymoon suite of an old Southern plantation that had been converted into a bed and breakfast, we spent a week on a quiet, Florida island. We basked in a private playground with sun-drenched waves and a Jacuzzi tub on the deck of our beach house overlooking the azure ocean — a perfect setting to embark on our deep exploration of one another.

During those days and many that have followed, this exploration has gone further, touching remote corners of each other's soul and probing into places we never dare to venture unless someone we profoundly trust coaxes us past our fears. Our emotional discoveries have been intricately intertwined with our journey into sexual intimacy.

The longer we are married and the more time I am allowed to ponder the life of Jesus, the more in awe I am of the implications that our love for each other is an invoking and actual offering of divine love. I have grown in wonder at what Paul seemed to be alluding to when he evoked the mystery of marriage.

In Ephesians 5, Paul continued his discourse on the practical outworking of his earlier admonition that the church, the believing community of faith, was no longer enslaved to their old, destructive life but was in fact now "alive with Christ." They were free to live in ways that reordered their world.[2] In Paul's thinking, the relationship between a husband and a wife was central to these ethical demands of the gospel. A careful parsing of Paul's writings leaves the distinct impression that the new community inaugurated in Jesus had at its core an enlivened (and in a certain sense recreated) union of man and woman.[3]

This union was a reflection of — perhaps a return to — our original design. God never intended for one he had created to live alone, removed from an intensely intimate connection with another human. The rugged individual needing no one and operating autonomously was never part of our DNA.

Though, admittedly, Creation was a cosmically huge and indescribable thing, the Bible's description of this event conveys a nearly predictable routine. God would display his creative powers by carving up a canyon, carefully hanging a galaxy in just the proper spot, or shuffling out one of his newly formed four-legged creatures. Then he would sit back with satisfaction and declare it "good."

This routine is why God's abrupt declaration surprises us. After breathing life into Adam, God offered the startling comment that something was amiss, something was "not good." It was not good, God declared, that Adam was alone, that he was the first — and only — of the created order that did not share intimacy with another of his same kind.[4]

All of creation reflected the reality of its Creator. Humankind was no different in this respect, and yet in a truly remarkable way, humanity was entirely different from the rest of creation. Humanity bore the significant distinction of being an image bearer of God himself. Humanity was designed to somehow carry with it, inherent in its very essence, something of God, a reflection of the Divine.

Theologians have sparred for generations about what it means precisely for a human to bear the image of God. What is it of God's nature that is intrinsically tied to being human? My guess is that we have only begun to understand this reality. However, the context of the early pages of Genesis where this image-bearing declaration is made appears to tell us this: Whatever else it might suggest, it most certainly means that we were intended to exist in community.

Immediately preceding his scooping of the earth's soil and crafting the form of a man, God spoke, apparently conversing with himself. His words echoed Trinitarian reality: "Let *us* make humanity in *our* image, after *our* likeness" (italics added).[5] The development of God's revelation as a three-in-one God is obviously far down the road from where this sits in Genesis. And if our only instruction regarding God's nature came from Genesis, we would have more questions than answers.

However, we do get the astonishing sense that God, self-contained as he was, eternally existent and the "one true God," somehow — amazingly — existed in what could be described as absolute perfect community. God did not create humanity out of some emotional deficiency, an anxious need for a relationship, or a desire for some distraction from boredom. God the Father was not bored with God the Son or God the Spirit.

Whatever additional implications are present in the affirmation of bearing God's image, at least this we know: We were created to mirror God—his very reality—by living in deeply connected relationship as God himself has always done. This reflection of God, this mirroring of God to the created world, is first expressed in the joining of man and woman. God's first expression of his image was the creation of male and female intended to live together, entirely immersed in one another, "one flesh." Together, they were a living symbol of God, an iconic appearance of God in his world.[6]

Man and woman, joined in spirit and body, were to literally display God. God has always been intent on incarnating himself into the human dominion, climaxed in the implausible event in which God actually *became* man in Jesus.[7] And here, in the opening pages of the God-story, we find a hint of this incarnational impulse. In the sinew and bone and emotional complexity of human intimacy, God is present, God is revealed.

It is possible to read these biblical assertions tamely or to sterilize them with cool theological detachment. We can use terms that are polite and sensible, toning down the evocative imagery. Yet the words of Genesis are not merely about the *institution* of marriage, the honorable, civil arrangement of a lifelong commitment between two orderly, responsible adults. Imbedded in the Genesis account, we find earthy sensuality. The writer is not timid. His words are tasteful, but they are clear. The man and woman literally become "one flesh." As Adam enters Eve and Eve receives Adam, there is no distinction between the realities of their spiritual oneness and their physical oneness. God does not draw the dichotomies we often do between the secular and the sacred, the physical and the spiritual. In their expressions of passionate physical union, they are not merely *demonstrating* their union. They are, in fact, *participating* in it.

Even in God's naming of his first human creations, we find sexual imagery. The grammatical root for the Hebrew *neqebah*, the term for female, is "pierced," and grammarians have noted that this word was applied to the feminine because of its descriptive quality.[8] Further, the etymology for *zakhar*, the Hebrew word for male, comes from the root notion of being "sharp" or "pointed."[9] Implanted in our very identity, our very name, are allusions to our sexuality. In Scripture, we find that sex is not just an act of pleasurable proportions. It is intertwined with our personhood.

Almost as if the author of Genesis wanted to be absolutely certain his sexual metaphors would not be missed, he offered the unblushing conclusion to the human creation account: "The man and his wife were both naked, and they felt no shame."[10] Completely naked, withholding nothing from one another, they were perfectly at rest, as safe as they were exposed. They were in perfect community, reflecting their Creator.

The prophet Malachi matched the sensuous speech in Genesis. In disbelief that God's people had so cavalierly ignored the reality of God in their midst, he questioned how the Israelite men could sleep with women other than their wives. This sin was serious because they had broken their covenant promises with their partners.

Evoking Genesis vocabulary, Malachi pointed to an even more serious breach in their sinful behavior: "Didn't God make you and your wife one?"[11] Malachi lodged the accusation with full force. How could they so easily disregard this powerful spiritual connection created by the very hand of God? The argument is, on many levels, focused on the sexual realm. Malachi's argument was that God had desired "godly offspring," fruit from their marital passion.[12]

Malachi punctuated his stern rebuke with an unusual, provocative assertion. "When God physically joined you and your wife as one," he asked, "wasn't the Spirit of God woven into that physical union?"[13] Malachi furthered the argument from Genesis: Something of God is uniquely present in the sexual expressions of a husband and a wife. How then, Malachi lamented, could this sacred space created for utter honesty, complete nakedness, and full giving of one's self to another be so defamed? How could the hallowed place where God's presence is abundantly alive and where his gift toward human pleasure so powerfully climaxes be so effortlessly disregarded?

Coming full circle to Paul, we find this same well-dug stream. Paul instructs wives and husbands to love and serve one another, grounding his admonitions in the love and sacrificial life of Jesus. Do as Christ did, Paul repeats. Appealing to Genesis for support, Paul insists his readers remember that God made them "one flesh."[14] Physically united. Raw. Sensuous. Sexual.

And then Paul says it, straightforward and remarkable. "This is a profound mystery," he says, "but I am talking about Christ and the church."[15] This physical union, this act of physical intimacy that plays a part in mirroring God's image to the world, is somehow another way of speaking about Christ, the second member of the Trinity, and of speaking about Christ's people, the community of the faithful. Profound mystery indeed.

Paul's words are unambiguous. He did not say the oneness of man and woman is a good example of Christ and the church. He did not say it was a nice reminder. His extraordinary proposition is that, in some way, speaking of physical oneness between husband and wife is the same as speaking of spiritual oneness between Jesus and the people for whom he died.

As a husband and wife surrender themselves to one another, intent on offering unselfish abandonment for the other's good and pleasure, they are granting a gift. It is a grace, generous and lavish. Paul tells us this moment of grace is an encounter inhabited by the life and reality of Jesus.

Much of the church speaks of sacraments.[16] The number of recognized sacraments may vary from one tradition to the next, and the precise interpretation of a given sacrament's purpose is often debated. But the central truth of sacraments is constant. A sacrament is a physical rite with which a spiritual reality is expressed.

Sacrament flows out of the Incarnation. God is intent on revealing himself in language we can understand and in forms we can on some level comprehend. God has wired humans to experience more than to theorize. We are a visceral clan. We need to touch, to taste, to smell. We need to rub our noses in the dirt and let the mist tickle our face. I can speculate on the energy and power of mass eruptive emotion, or I can stand in the middle of the pulsing crowd at a World Cup soccer event and feel my heart pound when the tightly pressed horde itches to stampede the field. There are some things you just can't grasp without rubbing up against the adrenaline and the chaos. You have to be in it, deep in it.

Sex is one of these places where we can get in it. If we truly opened our souls and fully embraced our nakedness, we would find ourselves acutely awake, alive. At first, our stirring might be only the obvious physical reactions as our bodies ache for our lovers. However, if we gave our nakedness time to take its course, we would find our physical responses, powerful and delightful as they are, opening windows to much deeper places of our souls. These deeper places call to us, but our humanness, our imperfect lives in an imperfect world, can keep us from discovering them. Though we are compelled to give ourselves fully to our partner, we tend to hold back much of ourselves — maybe out of fear, selfishness, or self-protection.

Thus, that which was intended by God — this deep, spiritual-sexual connection that speaks in God-language — is enjoyed incompletely. Our yearnings, raw as they are, invite us in. They speak to us, whispering words that stir life. But the stirrings are not always fulfilled. They offer a glimpse of more, but sometimes only a glimpse. Still, the God-written DNA compels us to seek it out, to hunger for it.

Nakedness, the fully exposed human body, is a treacherous power. It is an experience in redemption, a place where the wounds of sin and the Fall have the potential to find at least a hint of healing. In nakedness, we return to the Garden and attempt to give ourselves completely to another. Sometimes we wince at the sheer rawness of these moments. A steady gaze at our lover's body, despite how delighted we might be, can be overwhelming. Why is that? How can something as titillating as my wife's nakedness bring about in me the odd reaction of drawing back, dropping my gaze, or turning away, unsure and uncertain? Perhaps in that nakedness, that potential sexual connection, we sense the presence of God and are caught between what we know and what we don't understand.

Nothing is so human, so organic, as our sexuality. We are the only species possessing the capacity for nakedness. Plant life doesn't go nude. The animal kingdom has never known a streaker. When God placed us in his Garden, we owned nothing but our skin. We were buck naked and couldn't have been happier.

Embracing our bare selves is more than an exercise in quelling our inhibitions. It is a bold expression of the human soul seeking to be intensely alive and spiritually attuned. In a broken world where selfishness often trumps "giving fully" to anything other than self, this is a difficult goal to achieve. And it is made more difficult by the fact that the beauty of human nakedness and the arousal it entices has been taken over by pornographic exploitation and the sophomoric crudeness of frat-style humor. Ravaged as a tawdry marketing gimmick, sexuality is presented as a commodity you can purchase by the pound — and with coupons! In God's plan for sexual beauty, a trace of the Divine Presence is offered to us, but we disdainfully brush aside this sacramental subtlety in order to grab what we wrongly assume is the focus of our passions: the moment, the flesh, the greedy eagerness. Instead of gazing at the deep, true beauty, we take in the shadow.

Nurtured and explored in the context of marital community and coupling, nakedness can be an expression of God's presence, his design, his own handcrafted artistry. Knowing this, to gaze at the exposed, barren body of a lover is to admire something of God. To touch this body, to caress and explore it, is to touch something in the realm of the sacred.

The sages of old, from Elijah to Moses to Joshua, echo a firm caution for stepping onto hallowed ground frivolously. Uzzah, who simply reached out to grab the ark as it bounced on its buckboard cart, would assuredly warn us that touching the sacred, touching where God resides, is a terror.[17]

Yet we are invited — even compelled — toward this terror. We were made for enveloping the nakedness of our soul mates. Our hearts hope for it. Our souls yearn for it. Our bodies throb for it. We want to be intertwined with our lovers, experiencing ecstasy we can't describe and emotions we can't express. We sense something of eternity, something of Eden, something of God in that promise — whether we find it often, rarely, or even never.

With the grace of sexual oneness, the gospel is spoken. The redemptive words of God invade. In my wife's eyes, I see that I am desired, believed in, valued. I experience love. I taste it and smell it. I drown in it. It is the kind of love that is honest, fully divested, without reservation or demand. It isn't always, or even usually, this way. But I have had a taste, a small nibble. It has offered me life. I might run from it, forget it, or allow my selfishness to push me far from this sacred and pleasurable place, but there have been moments of such holy pleasure, moments I cannot deny.

This is not to say that only in marital coitus can the deepest truths of the gospel be experienced. The gospel is for the broken, the weak, the wounded, the disappointed — for all of us. All of us are tattered and scarred, weary and disillusioned. Some of us are oversexed, and we need the grace of sex restored. Some of us are undersexed, and we are desperate to have our longings fulfilled. Even these afflicted places, however — the yearning for more, the longing — speak of God.

If we are uncomfortable with such an earthy blending of the human and the Divine, it is my hunch that it is because we have an inadequate view of Incarnation. Incarnation makes the absurd assertion that the ripened sweat of a Galilean carpenter was the very sweat of God. Every ache and temptation and emotional discomfort Jesus experienced was God's experience. God is interwoven with his creation in ways that astound the pious and appear almost irreverent.

Mysteriously, sex is one of these sacred encounters through which God's life can flow and his grace can be received. In the erotic union, the common can become holy. I have come to think of sexual intimacy as the matrimonial Eucharist. The marriage bed is a place where heaven can touch earth.

Mike Mason has compared marital sexuality to prayer and to the spiritual embracing of death: "Like prayer, sex is a thing of exertion, sweat, and of groaning, and like death, it is intimately acquainted with surrender, and excretion, and with the mournful frailty and heartening glory of flesh."[18] How differently would we view our sexuality, imbibing in its pleasure and eschewing its selfish abuses, if we valued it for what it truly is: a place where God is, where God can speak?

Sex was fashioned, as Mason reminds us, "to instruct [us] in a higher nature, and in [our] destiny. For in touching a person of the opposite sex in the most secret place of his or her body, with one's own most private part, there is something that reaches beyond touch, that gets behind flesh itself to the place where it connects with spirit, to the place where incarnation happens."[19]

When I look deeply into my lover's eyes, I see things I can't explain and hear words that have never been spoken. In our bed of passion, I encounter realities that have previously hovered only as theories or ideals. If I listen, I can hear the heart of God. Wrapped in my lover's arms, I feel the embrace of God. In her eyes, I see love — untainted, tender, and open. This is why I must describe sex as a sacrament, a means of grace.[20]

Philip Yancey has described human sexuality as a rumor of the spiritual world. It is most certainly a provocative power we are unable to ignore. Doesn't this hint that it must speak deeply of God? We might twist it or abuse it, manipulate it or taint it. Yet there it is, drawing us, capturing us, reminding us that there are forces that transcend us, forces we can't control.

Might it even be that our innately human need for sex screams of our need for the One who created us as sexual creatures? "Throughout history," Marva Dawn writes in her book *Sexual Character*, "basic sexual desire has caused human beings to turn the need for affection and genital sexual expression into a god. . . . Our fundamental, intense longing for intimacy with God — part of the 'eternity' in our soul — is misunderstood as yearning for human intimacy. It isn't new that in our present epoch 'sex' should be one of the major idolatries."[21]

Some say our culture thinks of sex too much. I have come to believe our culture thinks of sex far too little. While it occupies a good bit of our collective energy and our private neurosis, we have a pitifully small view of sex. Sex is not primarily urges or arousals. It is not technique, and it is not ultimately defined by orgasm. Sex is a mysterious act of worship that whispers something of God to us.

CHAPTER 7

the deep waters of lament

Pain entered into, accepted, and owned can become poetry.

—EUGENE PETERSON

To pray with Jews means to stay as long as these poems do at the raw edge with a live God who will not let us settle easily or for too long.

—WALTER BRUEGGEMANN

"You have said harsh things against me."

—MALACHI 3:13

As much joy as there is to be found in sexual pleasure, reality tells us there is often far more pain. We hope for intimacy and shared delight, yet we often receive rejection or contempt. We feel used or empty. The ideal, good and true as it is, isn't always (or often, for some) met in these places outside the Garden. It seems almost cruel for Scripture to stir such hope and desire in us, only to see it mangled by disappointment. What do we do with this divergence between our hope and our experience?

As I explore Scripture, I find a brutality that unnerves me. Among its pages, words are spoken that seem out of place in a heavenly book. If I root around, stir up the dust, and really settle in with what I uncover, I am immersed in a frustrating disorientation. It agitates me. It rattles me. Yet it is strangely hopeful in a painful sort of way. Like a young, nervous bird flung from the high nest by its mother, I feel the adrenaline, the speed, the rush of destiny and newness, the terror. To fly is to live — it is what we all hope for. But the excruciating fling from safety, that is cruel.

There are many responses to the words and workings of God with which I am familiar, even comfortable. Obey. Serve. Repent. Trust. Believe. Hope. These concepts have been part of my spiritual lexis and regimen as long as I have been in the faith. They are biblically sound, and they represent imperative elements of the disciplined spiritual life.

However, left to themselves, these practices disintegrate into something brittle and lifeless. They are positive actions, and they can express a vigorous and committed faith in God. But as I read Scripture and experience the life about which Scripture speaks, I see how these actions can also be perverted to the unanticipated conclusion of squelching faith. Faith is that God-inspired tenacity to sludge through the grim and despairing stretches of our life, not by pretending they don't exist but by embracing the fear that comes in acknowledging their hideous subsistence and hoping against sane judgment that God is true and we aren't playing the part of the fool in believing that he is.

When faith is separated from its opportunity to connect with and emerge from the grieving, sorrowful, desolate places of the soul, our spiritual experience owns the proper words but misses much of the heart. Permitted to persist, this artificial separation will rob us of a great deal of our humanity and, to an even greater degree, it will rob us of some of the ways God intends for his created beings to interact with him.

If we silence our fears, deny the realities that pull against dutiful obedience, and refuse to allow ourselves to feel the emotions conflicting with our desire to hope and believe, then faith is denied its place. If we are not capable of acknowledging our dark suspicions because we are perplexed and unable to reconcile what we know of God's character with what we experience — the disconcerting, seemingly random ways God acts (or does not act) — then faith is again denied its place. There is no need for faith. We have managed to maneuver around it, and it dies.

When faith wilts, either by committing emotional suicide or by merely surrendering to our baffled reality, the result is the same: hollowness. For those of us who walk this pseudospiritual path, especially if we do so under a denial mistakenly labeled *obedience*, we disassociate from the very turmoil that would make our submission true, warm, and animated. We decline into a Christian experience mired in a dull conformity of dry joys and small dreams divorced from our heart. When the spiritual ideals of obedience and trust and hope are not augmented by the raw stuff of the human soul, something is quietly, though violently, surrendered. There are certain complicated, emotive experiences that are uniquely anthropomorphic, such as an honest grappling with grief and anger and fear, and when they are relinquished, the ideals become sterile and inhuman. They become nothing more than rigid activities performed to deny rather than wrestle through the knottiness of life.

A commitment to such a gaunt expression of these spiritual disciplines rejects life as it is, refuses to accept what is true. Obedience and faith mean little because in this illusionary world, there is nothing of import that would claw at our faith, nothing of significance that would suggest obedience might not be worthwhile. In this Pollyanna unreality, we reduce faith to trite ideals and simplistic postulations. We take a complex God and a perplexing world and reduce them to a bumper sticker or a T-shirt caption.

To counteract this addiction for ignoring the dark side of human experience and to fight to preserve both our hearts and our integrity, the Scriptures offer us the ancient practice of lament, complaining against God. The Scriptures, particularly many of the wisdom passages, are scandalous in how they model the spiritual discipline of wrangling with God. The Hebrews nurtured the discipline of lament to an art form. They understood the God-honoring and humanity-requiring need to recognize the deep brokenness of the soul — and to muster the courage to embrace it before God. To declare it to him. To shout or mumble it at him.

Much of the language used in the complaints flung at God is unsettling. It isn't how we suppose good, God-fearing folk should address the Almighty. I have been tempted to take one of David's more brazen rants — in which he passionately accuses God of not keeping up his end of the bargain or not doing a very good job of protecting his divine reputation — and mixing the language up a bit, making it fit my own vocabulary, personality, and context.

I have imagined standing up on a Sunday morning and unleashing it with passion and fury, as I expect it was originally expressed. I wouldn't speak in a slow or dignified cadence. I wouldn't enunciate my words with homiletic exactitude or pause for dramatic pastoral effect. I wouldn't use a calming tone to help tame the gravity of the shocking words being spoken. I wouldn't introduce the rant with a warning of its graphic or potentially unsettling content. I wouldn't plead with the hearers to stay with me to the end because if they would just hear me out, it would make better sense. I wouldn't close with a disclaimer or a cute story to attempt to soften the impact.

I would just stand in front of the people with my shirt half untucked and my hair rowdy and unkempt. I imagine myself, with a strange look in my eye that could pass for bewilderment but might just as easily pass for anger, vomiting my angst, my fear, my anger, my sorrow. After I'd finished, as I envision it playing out, I would stand there staring at the crowd, wild and sweaty and alive. I would stand there and say nothing, simply allowing the silence to eke as the uncertain crowd began to shift in their seats and look down at the floor or around the room or longingly at the back doors — anywhere but at me, that crazy man up front.

They might think I was inebriated or insane. They might think I needed a sabbatical — or as we like to put it kindly, "another place to serve and use my gifts." They would never, ever pause to consider that I had just quoted holy Scripture.

It's a great vision, a wonderful fantasy. But I won't do it. I'm too scared. I'm too dishonest. When it comes to laying my heart on the line and taking the notion of living with integrity deeper than emotional topsoil, I usually bail. David lives in a world I admire — from a distance. I enjoy reading David's words because it feels a little scandalous, like I've sneaked into the room of a friend's sister and pulled out her diary. David says things that make me tingle, that shake me up, that invite me to a place I have never been, an adventurous, daring, honest place.

But I won't follow. David might be bold and candid, but he's a crazy man.

When the psalmist locks horns with God, he holds nothing back. He doesn't try to placate or make sure he offers an appropriate number of niceties to counterbalance his strong demeanor. He just lets it rip. He tells God where he is, what he feels, and precisely what it is he is thinking, no matter how unsavory or libelous it might be. This stance is an act of sincerity, of owning up to the reality that hiding our hearts, particularly the bitter portions, doesn't mean they aren't there.

Larry Crabb says integrity is refusing to pretend about anything. I wonder if lament seems so foreign to me because I am not truly committed to a heart of integrity. Perhaps I am caught up in the world of pretend, where it is safe, where Humpty Dumpty is always put back together again, and where hobbits always make it back to the warm firesides of the shire. I can't lament because I can't admit that my world is broken, that my heart aches, or that neither I nor the ones I love are guaranteed safety.

Lament is terrifying.

Lament places a high value on truth telling, recognizing that to enjoy true love, we must know and be known. To know, however, is to give and receive vicious honesty that eschews denial, one of hiding's oldest forms. Love does not hide, not even those parts of us that are hideous and rancid, not even the words that are the hardest to say and even harder to hear. Love does not hide. Love does not lie. Sometimes, love laments.

Eugene Peterson invites God-followers to honest acts of lament, knowing that untruths are worse than what we fear most: pain. He says, "Put form and rhythm and song to [your pain]. Pain isn't the worse thing. Being hated isn't the worst thing. . . . Death isn't the worst thing. The worst thing is failing to deal with reality and becoming disconnected from what is actual. The worst thing is trivializing the honorable, desecrating the sacred."[1]

Laments are spoken out of disorientation. They emerge when we have hit the wall, been utterly ruined, and had our hopes ripped up and thrown to the wind. They lurch from our gut when God has gone AWOL, when our darkest suspicions appear to be true: God doesn't exist — or worse, he is there, but he doesn't care in the least. From this wretched place, lament seeps. It spills out of our souls and forms a dark, muddy puddle at our feet. Lament gives us words to attach to our chaos. "The Psalms," says Walter Brueggemann, "offer speech when life has gone beyond our frail efforts to control it."[2]

What is most difficult about biblical lament, however, is whom we target with our untethered emotion: God. This spewing at the Creator doesn't jive with most of what I have been taught about my pursuit of spiritual intimacy with God. It would be rare for me to have the emotional integrity to speak such honest words to my wife or to a friend; it would be antithetical to my long-molded character to even consider such a conversation with God.

Brueggemann reminds me how far my situation has drifted from my spiritual forefathers. "Most of the lament psalms," he says, "are the voices of those who 'are as mad as hell and are not going to take it anymore.' They are not religious in the sense that they are courteous or polite or deferential. They are religious in the sense that they are willing to speak this chaos to the very face of the Holy One."[3]

The Hebrews who heard Malachi's prophetic voice had no problem lobbing complaints at God. They were dismayed and bitterly disappointed. Some of them were angry. They believed they had done their part — keeping the law, remembering the sacrifices, performing their perfunctory religious duties. But God hadn't done his part. He had reneged on the deal. Rain hadn't come. The crops were shriveled and crusty. And worse, the pagans, the "evildoers" as they put it, were prospering. Bad as it was that they who named Yahweh as their God were suffering, it was far worse that those who derided God *weren't*. Nothing ups the ante on misery like a little jealousy.

And they let God hear about it. *What difference does it make if we follow after you? We might as well run after the other gods for all you care. Serving you is a waste.*

I expect God to respond in fury, to come unhinged. My macabre eagerness moves forward, expecting some eruptive action, perhaps a nice earthquake to remind them who's boss or a series of well-aimed lightning bolts to put the fear of God back in them. God's response, however, is measured. He acknowledges their incriminating protests with a prickly reply: "You have said harsh things against me."[4]

It appears there were at least two groups of people expressing their testy grievances to God. One was a voracious bunch whose only interest in God was in how they could use him. They were chafed not because their hopes had been dashed but because their greedy schemes hadn't panned out. For them, God had committed the ultimate sin: He had cost them a buck.

I see myself among this greedy lot. More often than I care to admit, God is a means to an end. I want a good marriage, healthy kids, a meaningful and fulfilling career, a decent vacation each year, and a generous dose of satisfaction along the way. I expect a few bumps, a disappointment here and there; but on the whole, I require smooth sailing. And God is going to give it to me.

The second group, however, despaired from a different place. They were shell-shocked, in disarray. Their world had gone topsy-turvy. Their faith had worn thin not because their gluttonous desires had been thwarted but because their sense of God had been overturned. What they had always believed to be true about God—that he was good and would come through for them if they would just follow his instructions—didn't seem certain anymore.[5]

Most of us are familiar with this disheartened clan. If we have believed in God for any length of time, we have felt the prick of disappointment. We might have ignored it, chalked it up to a simple misunderstanding, or avoided it altogether by throwing all our passion at our next hope, our next big plan. But if we are honest, somewhere along the way we have seen hopes fizzle as God refused to play his assigned role in our carefully staged play.

The complaints of this latter group appear to be audacious, if not bumbled, attempts to wrestle with their disillusionment, to goad God into some kind of response. Their world had unraveled, and they were desperate to get God's take on it no matter what it required.

And so these groups spoke these harsh words, and God's judicious response recognized their two very different realities. To those who were egocentric and bothered only by God's failure to deliver what they demanded, he spoke judgment. To those who were despondent and expressed the honest rue of their souls, he spoke hope. For God, complaint and accusation—even directed at him—is not out of bounds. Emotional dishonesty (manipulatively twisting God's arm for selfish purposes) and a fragmented perception of reality (imprudently believing God is here for our purposes rather than our being here for his), however, God will always call foul.

Biblical lament speaks to both realities: the arrogant attempt to use

God and the painful wounds of being disappointed by him. Lament places people of both situations squarely before God, inviting us to the rawness of engaging God for who he is, not who we have imagined him to be. This is the simple power of lament — it is a nakedly honest engagement with God.

This Godward direction of lament is what makes it holy, what makes it powerful — ultimately, what makes it a bold step of faith. Faith is evidenced in the fact that the lament is directed toward God. It is not neat or tidy. It can be harsh and abrasive, unnerving and bitter. It is not even always true.[6] But it is a sacred act because it takes God seriously.

We have placed a premium on the dull and the lifeless. Disengaged obedience has somehow ascended to the place of high spiritual experience. Dull, lifeless devotion is seen as a virtue. God is never seriously questioned. We never yell at him. We never wrangle with him. I wonder if we really love him.

Miska wants to see me angry. She wants me to throw something, maybe even cuss a little. She wants to see my blood boil. She wants me to argue and refuse to back down. She wants to know I am alive. Emotions come in bundles, and rarely can we turn off one without turning off the whole bunch. She wants all of me, even the nasty parts.

So brutal lament is an act of faith and love. We are refusing to give up on God, refusing to succumb to the fears that he isn't there or will never listen. When we speak our anger toward God, we are saying that we believe he is bigger than us, that he can handle us — all of us, even our wildest emotions. When we give ourselves over to honesty and tell God we aren't sure he exists, we are, in a paradoxical roundabout, proclaiming exactly the opposite: our deepest conviction, perhaps even our most unverifiable axiom, that God is alive and well. If we speak from our honest places of desolation and doubt and give them to God, they are acts of faith.

To invite such lament is not to suggest that any form of expression toward God is desirable. As I work through these tensions, I struggle. God can handle any of our emotions, and it is always better to take them to him than to hide them under some ruse of detached faithfulness. Lament will at times head outside the bounds of how we would hope to feel toward God, even beyond what might in fact be true about God.

Biblical lament is a faithful act because it is a way of staying in God's story, a way of integrity — disturbing as it might be — that refuses to veil our most grief-filled anxieties and confusions. However, some forms of sorrow or anger are merely ways of disconnecting, controlling, or demanding. I have noticed that some of my untamed emotional outbursts toward God are not offered as appeals for hope that God will show himself faithful but as a rigid demand that God meet up to my expectations — or else. Lament should not be used merely as an excuse to vent, to dismiss our responsibility to deal with God. Sometimes what we might pass off as lament is really only a childhood temper tantrum in which we pound the floor and flail our legs in the air with preadolescent drama in hopes that when the chaos we have caused passes, we can go about playing with our toys as we had wanted to all along. Lament is not a trick.

Experience every emotion. Bring every fiber of rage and grief and agony to God. But bring it to *God*. Engage him. This is what makes lament true and healthy, an act of worship. The lament of the Scriptures is respectful of God as the only One to whom we can go. God as God — this is the start and the finish. And all the doubt and grief and wrangling fill the space in between.

If we scorn these faithful and disturbing expressions, if we are too uncomfortable, too fearful, or too disconnected from our fears and pains to recognize they exist, we run the risk of missing God.

Odd, isn't it, that some of the very things we have been told would pull us from God are the things the Scriptures suggest will save us? This is why Brueggemann bemoans speech that is "dulled and mundane." He mourns the fact that "our passion has been stilled and without imagination. Often the Holy One is not addressed, not because we dare not, but because God is far away and hardly seems important."[7] Lament respects God far too much to lie. Lament runs after God, even if in unorthodox ways, to offer him an honest soul.

The wisdom writers and the prophets tell us to take God seriously, to engage him with our whole being. We have to unlearn some of what we might believe about God and faith to embrace this path. We have to listen to Scripture, to be open to the offbeat voice of the Spirit, to help one another learn the language of our heart and allow it to express itself in the language of lament.

Peterson encourages us to "teach one another how to take seriously these great cadences of pain, some coming from hate, some coming from love, so that we're not diminished but are deepened by them — find God in them, and beauty."[8]

Last year my family and I came back from a week at the beach. When we walked into our house, we were met with a phone call. A friend had been killed in a biking accident. As he was riding on a winding, country road, a truck hauling concrete tried to pass him. When I went to the scene, the police markings told the gruesome story.

It shouldn't have been. Aaron was young and single. He loved God.

He gave his life and his resources to God's purposes. He served. His whole life was ahead of him. It didn't make sense. From my vantage, God had not acted Godlike. He had not protected Aaron. He had not done right by my friend.

I doubted God. It forced to the surface some of my darkest questions about him. I had a choice: I could hide, crawling in a corner until the pain numbed and a small portion of my heart died, or I could lament.

I wrestled with a paradox. My addiction toward trying to control chaos propelled me to question whether God's claim of sovereignty could be maintained during such tragedies. If his control was so capricious and unwieldy, better to let me handle the job. At the same time, the only release I could find from my turmoil was to cling, by faith alone, to the simple reality that somehow, despite the unpredictability of God's interventions, he was, in fact, boss.

These were my words:

> *O God,*
> *I say you are in control, sovereign.*
> *The Scriptures seem to suggest you are.*

> *Today I wonder.*

> *I wonder how your control could oversee the destruction*
> *we have experienced this weekend,*
> *The emptiness*
> *The darkness*
> *The loss*
> *The carnage of our hearts.*

Your control has seen fit to leave parents empty,
    Friends alone
    A church community in despair
    The hurting and helpless and destitute with one less
        advocate in this horrific world.

It seems this tragedy is nothing but evil
    Nothing but chaos run wild
    Nothing but another moment of heartbreak and fears
        coming true.

Yet I declare again, at moments even reluctantly, that
        you are in control, sovereign.
    I have nowhere else to turn
    None other in whom to hope.

Now, in this place, I do not ask you to make sense of
what has occurred — that seems a mockery.

I ask you to be what I believe, in faith, you are:
    In Control.
    Sovereign.
    God.

Amen.

These words were not easy. They didn't make me feel good. But they were honest. They were acts of faith. I was even able to end the lament with an expression of trust. God didn't teach me much through this experience. I think it would be arrogant of me to think he would. There were many others who felt the loss of Aaron more deeply than I. But I experienced something of God in these words that I could have missed (as I often have) if I had not responded to the prompting to meet God in the mystery.

CHAPTER 8

whisper of pleasure

*What is it, then, that this desire [for happiness] . . .
proclaim[s] to us, but that there was once in man a
true happiness of which there now remain[s] to him
only the mark and empty trace.*

—BLAISE PASCAL

*The only people for me are the mad ones, the ones who
are mad to live, mad to talk, mad to be saved, desirous
of everything at the same time, the ones who never
yawn or say a commonplace thing, but burn, burn,
burn, like fabulous yellow roman candles exploding
like spiders across the stars.*

—JACK KEROUAC

"Yours will be a delightful land."

—MALACHI 3:12

Does God enjoy cartoons? I never thought I would be
accosted with such a philosophical dilemma. It was Monday
night, and I had just finished the second of five sessions I would be

leading at a Christian college. To open a conversation dealing with human desires and how Jesus on several occasions was determined to breathe passionate air into musty, passionless hearts, I showed a clip from *Finding Nemo* — the scene in which Marlin, the dad clown fish, meets up with Crush, the sea turtle. It is a fun scene in which Crush's childlike passion is humorously displayed, and whenever I show it, the groans that follow the click of the stop button let me know those in the audience would rather watch the rest of the movie than listen to me finish my talk. It's humbling.

Soon after I stepped away from the platform, a somber, husky fellow asked me to step away from the group so he could talk to me privately. I was glad to do so. His brusque tone and dull demeanor made me think he was struggling intensely and perhaps wanted to confess something to a stranger. Perhaps he wanted me to be his Father Joe. I was wrong.

When he had me in the corner of the room, he bluntly asked how I could laugh and jest at one moment and then speak of deep devotion to God in another. He asked how I could possibly condone using humor and wit to proclaim something as serious and foreboding as God's truth.

Apparently, God doesn't speak through animation. Talking fish and surfer-slang turtles are off-limits. "God doesn't laugh," he said, "except at the destruction of the wicked."

I have numerous problems with this brooding theology, but one of the most heinous, as I see it, is the notion that God doesn't laugh. He doesn't smile. He doesn't enjoy. He has no passion. The God this fellow proclaims seems dead to me.

Extreme as this experience is, such dull and destructive thoughts about God abound. God is often viewed as cold and emotionless, drained of surging desire and erupting vigor. The only passions God displays are the kind you would expect from one of Dickens' demented schoolmasters.

No beauty. No heat. Just drab. Wooden. Nothingness.

If this is how we imagine our Creator, then it is no surprise that our bland existence could be supposed a noble spiritual pursuit. Thankfully, the Scriptures do not proclaim such a God. And once we make this shift — from a dour, gloomy God to a God who is romantic, inspired, whimsical, poetic — it forces us to wrestle with how we view our own existence.

As ones created in God's image, we have a yearning for pleasure infused in us. We want it. We need it. We seek it. And we will find it somehow, somewhere — anywhere.

We cannot help but seek pleasure. To deny it is to resist *being*, to resist living. To not desire pleasure is like an attempt to stop breathing. The only way to finally halt the rhythm is to die.

There is, of course, the wildly popular dilemma fancifully termed *theodicy*. If a good God reigns over the universe, how can there be so much evil, so much pain in the world? The question deserves to be asked. However, there is another question that is equally as perplexing and receives far less attention. What about pleasure? Why do we enjoy? Why do we revel? Why do art and beauty and achievement and sex give us such intense delight?

It was precisely this question — How do we account for pleasure? — that hounded G. K. Chesterton during his search for personal significance. He found no satisfactory answer until he embraced belief in a creative God who desires his creatures to savor the world as he does. He explains it this way:

I felt in my bones; first, that this world does not explain itself. . . . There was something personal in the world, as in a work of art . . . [and] the proper form of thanks to it is some form of humility and restraint: we should thank God for beer and Burgundy by not drinking too much of them. . . . And last, and strangest, there had come into my mind a vague and vast impression that in some way all good was a remnant to be stored and held sacred out of some primordial ruin. Man had saved his good as Crusoe saved his goods: he had saved them from a wreck.[1]

Chesterton came to believe that human experiences of pleasure were remnants from the wreck. They were signs of what once was in Eden and what still is discovered when one is restored to God. And these signs, he would suggest, these pangs for enjoyment, turn us in the direction of the most profound realities about ourselves and our God.

We were created for desire. Our hearts were intended to be roused by pleasure. We can rebuff it. We can shun it. We can make our most determined effort to theologize it away. We can seek to kill it. But rest assured, it will not die.

Pleasure is a powerful apologetic because it is common to us all. Deep in our soul, there is a yearning for the transcendent, for the ineffable experience affirming that our humanness is more than a biological feat, an evolutionary triumph. We long to feel. We crave to be alive, truly alive.

Why do certain seemingly insignificant experiences evoke such warmth in us? The sweet smell of mist, the sound of crickets on a clear evening, the bright, fuzzy moon on a cloudy autumn night, a simple touch from our lover after a week apart — how can these everyday experiences touch our souls?

The particulars vary, but each of us knows such spaces, such smells, such people. Something stirs. There's a spark. At least for a moment, and sadly, often only for a moment, we are caught in the feel of the thing. We don't control it; we merely surrender to the happening. It is fresh. The moment is pregnant with vitality and audacity. The world offers hope again. It's hard to put words to this moment, but we all know it. Perhaps we could find a better word to describe its elusive essence, but for now, *pleasure* will have to do. All of us know pleasure. We might not have a language for it, but we know it all the same. Pleasure offers many angles. It's a slippery notion, to be sure. Delight. Titillation. Bliss. Amusement. Gusto. Indulgence. Each attempt to describe pleasure offers us something of the whole but never the whole.

Blaise Pascal muses how God uses both pain and pleasure to speak to his creatures. Pain pierces us. It slices into our most raw places and leaves us open, wounded, and desperate. Into this forlorn condition, we sit in the rare place called silence. And in this silence, this despair, God can often speak words we would not have listened to before. In the affliction, we see worlds and people and truths that our comfortable existence hid from us. I once asked a pastor I respect how it is his heart stays alive. "Through pain," he said. It wasn't the answer I was looking for, yet it has rung true.

But God also speaks through pleasure. It is rarely a loud speaking. It is more like a hint, a whisper. There are some things you can describe with words, and there are some things you can only point toward.

Pleasure seems to be God's way of pointing.

Pleasure is a way of experiencing, of having something wash over us. We can study a recipe for blackberry cobbler, memorizing its ingredients and fastidiously noting each step in the process. When the baking is finished, we can measure the thickness of the crumbling crust and compare the tint of the golden top to other cobblers we have known. Or we can stick our face in it, dead center. We can stuff warm berries in our mouths and lick buttery flakes of crust from our lips. Pleasure is something you just have to get all over you, something you have to stick your face in and taste.

For Pascal, *happiness* is a synonym for pleasure.[2] It's a plain word, happiness. It's overused and flattened with excessive wear. Yet somehow it works. Pascal insists that a pining for happiness is the hint of God lingering in every soul. It is common to human experience, a universal dialect.

"All men seek happiness," Pascal says. "This is without exception. Whatever different means they employ, they all tend to this end. The cause of some going to war, and of others avoiding it, is the same desire in both, attended with different views. The will never takes the least step but to this object. This is the motive of every action of every man, even of those who hang themselves."[3]

Even a suicide, he suggests, is an appeal to pleasure, an appeal to a morosely held belief that what will be found on the other side of the final breath is preferable (more pleasurable) to what is experienced on this side.

If a craving for pleasure is stitched into the human soul, how does this enlighten us? In what direction does this wind blow? It is my belief that our steady pull, our ravenous need even, to savor the sensual tells us something of our creation, something of who we are or, perhaps more directly, *whose* we are.

In the Genesis narrative, we find a wild and radically creative God living out of passion, out of desire. He had no deficiency, nothing he needed or required. He possessed no motivation to act other than what is most obvious: his desire to do so. God was knee-deep in creative work because he wanted to be. He didn't have bills to pay, and he didn't have overbearing parents pushing him into the family business of creating new worlds. God did what he wanted to do. God created for pleasure — his pleasure.

God loves beauty, so he fashioned hills and rugged terrain and antelope and cantaloupe and humans and zebras and marmot and anteaters. He loves change and variety, so he made swamplands and the Sahara Desert. He was passionate about those things that brought him pleasure.[4]

God finds great pleasure in what he has created, in all he has crafted around him. The psalmist tells us that God rejoices in his works.[5] He revels in them. He gets giddy over them. He laughs and marvels and pauses to take his creation in. He sighs with satisfaction. There are moments when his creative energy is so explosive, so *good*, that the only appropriate response is to rest. God rests. He savors. He puts down the brush and just drinks in the wonder.

In God's creative act, he infused into the human soul a bit of his own relishing in pleasure. However, this is the tragedy: Ever since paradise was lost, we have ignored the hints of God, the whisper of the Divine quietly murmured by our unquenchable desires. We have foolishly supposed that desire is something that tells us more about ourselves than our Maker.

And so in the hunt for pleasure, we run to the places it can never be found. We search and we dig. We fight and we steal. We run and we run and we run. And we always come up short.

Pascal continues,

> [God] only is our true good, and since we have forsaken him, it is a strange thing that there is nothing in nature which has not been serviceable in taking His place: the stars, the heavens, earth, the elements, plants, cabbages, leeks, animals, insects, calves, serpents, fever, pestilence, war, famine, vices, adultery, incest. And since man has lost the true good, everything can appear equally good to him, even his own destruction.[6]

When authentic pleasure is allayed, either by attempting to suppress its rumbling in our hearts or by sprinting after those places where pleasure will never be found, something in our souls shrivels. Unfortunately, the church has not always been a defender of pleasure. In well-meaning attempts to turn the cultural tide or call adherents to a moral code, we have squelched the raw elements of our humanity, the places within us where desire is ignited and passions are unleashed. The places where pleasure erupts.

The experiment has yielded disastrous effects. We might nurture a movement that is moderately more ethical or decent or conscientious, but we as a people are cold and aloof, dead. We might achieve an environment that is neat and tidy, never messy, and that is cautious and serious, never foolish. But for all our talk of life, can anyone really say we are *living*? We are safe, no doubt. But we lack any of the heat and the danger that signal life — messy, unbridled life.

God never intended such chilled and muted living. He created us like himself — for pleasure, to feel deeply, to live. This is why G. K. Chesterton likened the journey into God's story to a romance.[7] It awakens our hearts in ways we didn't know possible. It makes us silly. It makes us do goofy high-schoolish things, such as writing graffiti, staying up all night, and eating two dozen donuts just because we can. It makes us feel our hearts beat fast when those eyes across the room glance our way. It makes us write things that are sure to embarrass us later. It makes us giggle. It makes us cry. It makes us fling plates across the room in outbursts of passionate anger. It makes us feel.

This seems the best way to describe pleasure: giving occasion and space and respect to what is most alive in us, to that surge that reminds us we aren't yet dead. I believe it is then that we most clearly see God. Augustine taught that for a good Christian, all of life is an exercise of holy desire. True desire is a place where God resides.

Scattered across the centuries, there have been a few prophetic voices who have taught us such things. Malachi was God's messenger delivering a severe word to the people. However, as was true of most of the messengers through which God chose to speak, he exercised a steady appeal to the human desire to delight and revel in pleasure. Malachi enticed the people with images of overflowing crops, lavish wealth, and an abundance of grapes, which served as symbols of prosperity, joy, and gladness. He told the people that God would "throw open the floodgates of heaven and pour out so much blessing that you will not have room enough for it."[8] Malachi pronounced that they would find themselves a delightful people. *Delight*. A beautiful word.

Before Malachi finished his oracle, he offered an image strange to the modern eye and ear. Painting a vivid picture of a life abandoned to God, his final brushstroke offered that they would "go out and leap like calves released from the stall."[9] He was saying life with God is like a calf that leaps, a calf that has gorged itself on the finest grain and is released to playfully dance a calf-styled dance across the warm, sweet meadow.

These are not dour words. This is no heavy appeal to diligence or responsibility or even gratitude. This is an invitation to taste what is delicious and to feel what is sensuous. These are words ripe with pleasure.

Yesterday I took Wyatt and Seth for a walk. Well, I walked; they rode. We have a double stroller, one of those monstrosities the size of a small Yugo. You know your stroller has gotten out of hand when it has its own luggage rack and individual cup holders. It was a fantastic afternoon. Fall had just begun to tease, and the air was clean. It was a good time to take the boys outside.

Whenever we venture anywhere outside our cul-de-sac, however, it is serious business. There is no such thing as a leisurely saunter. It is more like an attempt to peak Mount Kilimanjaro. One hundred yards from our driveway, the road dips and then begins to climb. The upward angle is treacherous. When I used to run it alone, I appreciated the way it made my heart pound and my thighs burn. I would grimace and grit my teeth, but I knew I was working it good.

Now, shoving two boys and the inert Yugo up the incline, I began doing the math in my head to determine when both of the boys will be able to climb this hill on their own. On our way back, we neared the top of the hill, which on the return trip offers a harrowing descent. It is all the more exciting when I am attempting to hold back the forward momentum of the stroller and fifty pounds of eager, wide-alive-with-boyish-frenzy yells to "go faster!"

Wyatt sits in the back of the stroller, and yesterday he found a new way to increase the thrill. He held the seat in front of him for balance, pushed with his feet against the bottom of the stroller, and projected his body upward like Jack on the front of the Titanic. I was racing down the hill, holding on to the stroller with my best attempt at a firm grip with both hands while Wyatt arched his neck, thrust his head into the wind, and embraced speed like it was his favorite friend.

Between strides, I caught a glimpse of Seth in the front of the stroller, leaning forward as far as he could reach. Straining the harness strapping him in, he pounded on the plastic tray in front of him as if by hitting just a little harder, he might be able to coax a bit more velocity out of his plummeting ride.

Between laughing screeches, Wyatt screamed, "Faster, Daddy. Faster!"

Wyatt and Seth have not been trained in pleasure grabbing. They have not been taught the benefits of experiencing delight. They simply embrace what is alive in them, what calls their name. They will not be turned away; they rush headlong into it.

We might be tempted to shrink back, to think such an opening to pleasure conflicts with the truly spiritual pursuit. C. S. Lewis challenges such concerns. He suggests that our problem is not that we want too much pleasure but that we don't want enough. For Lewis, if we really gave pleasure its rightful place, if we truly insisted on having it — all of it — and flatly refused to be turned from it, then we would scoff at the smaller and more trivial asides. We would give little time to all that is antipleasure, which to Lewis means all that is anti-God.

John Piper has been a recent voice echoing similar words. He puts it plainly when he says the life to which we are called is a life of Christian hedonism. *Hedonism* might raise an eyebrow, but it couldn't be more appropriate. Sometimes you have to fiddle with people's vocabulary to grab their attention and help them hear. Words with zest can turn bland because they are left out in the open so long that much of the flavor dries up.

Pleasure can be such a word. It's a cute word. It's safe. *Hedonism* — now, that's a word we have to stand up for. It's a word that won't let us nudge by without at least stopping for a conversation.

Maybe this is why we miss much of God — maybe we have learned how to nudge past his words, to lower our head and stroll on past what he's doing right in the middle of us. Pleasure, creation tells us, is something he is doing right in the middle of us.

With pleasure, we either embrace it or we try to silence it. It's too painful to be anywhere in between. But how do we silence something that's ingrained into the truest part of who we are? We can't really stifle such a force. The only real option seems to be to drown it out, to clang away at something else so that the song of pleasure is muffled.

This incessant clanging is what Scripture and the church call sin. Sin is the relentless addiction to create meaning outside of God, to mute his music and attempt to create our own instead. Sin is the absurd assertion that life — and pleasure — can be found outside of God. Jeremiah the prophet likened it to digging wells where no water could ever be found. Augustine would refer to it as an utter human blindness to all that is true and to all that is life.

Yet the irony is that even in our sin, we cannot escape the voice of God. I am not merely saying that God speaks louder than our sin, true as that is. I am saying something more. God is so infused into the human experience that his voice echoes even in places that by their mere existence attempt to undermine his reality. The apostle Paul tells us that God is the One who holds all things together, and if we take Paul seriously, this would include even our sin, our rebellion, our numbing attempts to drown out his steady coaxing to embrace pleasure. Only God could take the very thing that curses all that he is and use it as his mouthpiece.

Thomas Aquinas spoke much of pleasure. He gave it a high place in his thinking, and he concluded that there was a remarkable link between the beauty of desire and the treachery of sin. For Aquinas, sin was the result of a good desire gone bad, a healthy, God-implanted yearning for pleasure twisting in the wrong direction to find its satisfaction.[10]

Aquinas seems to be echoing some of Paul's conversation in Romans. In Paul's struggle against the evil that plagued him, he was not frustrated because his desires toward evil were so pervasive; rather, he was profoundly disenchanted with why he could not more consistently align his actions that were so often turned toward vice with his desires that were oriented toward goodness. Paul wondered why his good desires did not more radically alter his experience. He wanted his desires to speak more loudly, to throw their weight around more forcefully.[11]

From the beginning, our passions and pleasures, our desires and ecstasies were all acts of worship, offered up to a God who received glory from our free and uninhibited expressions of beauty and ravenous living. But then came the Fall, the Great Tragedy, and humanity turned from God.

Yet even in the turning, we could not submerge our longing to experience enchantment, to feel pleasure. And so we set off to find it wherever it might be found, regardless of the cost or who we hurt along the way. We ravaged and plundered, connived and seduced and maneuvered. Pleasure simply must be had.

In our manic lusting and frantic searching, however, we seldom pause to notice the obvious irony. Our sin, our rebellion against all that is true in God, is a most vivid reminder of his presence. Our appetite speaks of longings so human, so profoundly resonant with our deepest selves that they hint at realities of the soul. Beauty, exploration, sexuality — these are universally desired.

And when we encounter these moments — a breathtaking view from atop a fourteen-thousand-foot peak, a jaunt into the art district of a city we have never experienced, a candlelit night of heart-drenched passion with our lover — something long submerged trembles. It rises up and grabs our breath. It whispers to our soul.

God is what it says.

It tells us we were made for such moments, such life. We were created for a Garden, crafted for delight. Seldom as we might experience it, ecstasy is not foreign to us. It is like an old friend whose unplanned return reminds us that something of ourselves has been missing. We have forgotten a piece of who we are. And we begin to see that we have been trying to make up for what has been missing in ways that now seem foolish.

This is how sin points us toward God, how it whispers his name. When I crave power, the craving is not the malefactor. The evil is my sickly attempt to fill the hollowness my craving exposes by seizing whatever I can grasp rather than turning to the One who enlivens my quest for meaning and reorders the attention of my desires toward ends that are true and good.

When I find my body yearning for a woman who is not my soul mate, it is not the yearning or the impulse toward sexual intimacy that is the villain. Rather, the beast to be tamed is the dark falsehood that my soul and my body will ever find what it properly aches for apart from the woman who owns my heart and who is truly able to open her body and soul to mine.

C. S. Lewis made a strong argument that pleasures "are shafts of the glory as it strikes our sensibility."[12] Pleasure is what happens when the Divine communicates with the human. Knowing that such affirmations would inevitably lead to obvious questions, he addressed whether there were such things as "bad, unlawful pleasures." "Certainly there are," he offered, "but in calling them 'bad pleasures,' I take it we are using a kind of shorthand. We mean 'pleasures snatched by unlawful acts.' It is the stealing of the apple that is bad, not the sweetness. The sweetness is still a beam from the glory."[13]

This sweetness — our cravings and our yearnings — yanks our attention toward a pleasure-giving God. Yet rather than sensing the thirst for pleasure, feeling its tingling sensation and its tender, wild invitation, we often seek to kill it. We quote a verse or divert our attention to something lesser, something smaller. We drink in the guilt of a feeling that never should have been. And, I believe, God's whispering heart is saddened as we deny the very essence of himself within us.

Pleasure is dangerous, and we often believe it is better to kill it altogether than to run the risk of pleasure run amuck. But as our experience suggests, it will not be killed. It might retreat for a moment.

It might release its demand for a time. But pleasure will not die. It can't.

Generations of spiritual experience tell us that what Dallas Willard calls the "gospel of sin management" (the assumption that moral behavior and merely "doing the correct thing" is God's ultimate end for his creation) does not yield spiritual life.[14] Rather, it yields a breeding ground for false pleasures, for forces that offer a bit of the thrill of pleasure without the fully immersed experience.

Thankfully, the Spirit does not go silent. He invites us to revel, to embrace, to feel. For in the reveling and the embracing, God has our attention. Lewis attempted "to make every pleasure into a channel of adoration,"[15] and imbibing God-saturated pleasure is one way we worship.

Our heart was created for such worship, and it will not be ignored forever. There is a profound beauty continuing to hint that we were created for something more.

CHAPTER 9

between

It's not dark, but it's getting there.

— BOB DYLAN

There's a place between here and there. A piece of ground in the middle of take-off and landing. A section of the unknown within beginning and ending. You probably find yourself there from time to time. It's the land known as Inbetween.

— MARGARET FEINBERG

Dear God, why are you invisible?

— ALEXANDRIA, AGE SIX

How have you loved us?

— MALACHI 1:2

As Malachi's message neared its conclusion, the prophet had great interest in helping the people get a fuller view of their historical situation. God had said, "Remember the law of my servant Moses, the decrees and laws I gave him at Horeb for all

Israel."[1] Malachi turned their gaze backward to their history, to their collective memory of what once was.

God had spoken. God had promised. Stories of Sinai, fiery clouds, water gushing out of rocks, and food falling from the sky had been recounted for generations. Their feasts recalled God's acts. Their festivals celebrated the memories. Even their vocabulary reflected words rich with recollections of how their God had intervened on their behalf. *Passover* elicited a sense of promise and salvation. *Manna* evoked images of miraculous care and divine intervention.

Refusing to allow them to linger in the past, however, the prophet abruptly insisted they look forward, remembering what God had promised would be. God had said he would again send Elijah the prophet.[2] The Israelites probably had little sense of what exactly it meant for Elijah to return, but they believed that with this future coming, somehow all that was wrong in their world would finally be set straight.[3]

By insisting they look simultaneously to the past as well as to the future, Malachi highlighted the reality of where they found themselves in that moment: hunkered down in the middle ground. They sat *in between*. They were in between hope and fulfillment, in between grasping after and grabbing on, in between what Robert Benson calls "the dreaming and the coming true."[4]

Centuries would unroll between the messianic promise in the Mosaic covenant and the time when the Messiah, the God-man Jesus, would fulfill the hopes the covenant had inspired. In these unfolding centuries, there was waiting and hoping and forgetting and wondering if they had all been fools, if Moses had been mistaken. Maybe there really wasn't anything to hope for after all.

Ironically, those who first received Malachi's oracle did not know the gravity of Malachi's in-between message. They would have to live through their unfolding history before they would be able to look back and recognize the veracity attached to the dire prediction the prophet gave.

Malachi teetered on a precipice, on the outer edge of an era. For centuries, God's utterances would be muted. His voice that at times had thundered and at other times had whispered would go silent. Imbedded in Malachi's closing words was the forewarning of an eerie reality the people would shortly encounter. Soon, the Voice that had offered both rebuke and comfort would offer neither. They stood on the verge of a laconic age.[5]

God is a speaking God—if nothing else, the presence of the Christian Scriptures tells us at least this much. Malachi's allusion to Horeb (also known as the "mountain of God") is a subtle reminder that God often is vocal. On Horeb, Moses heard God's voice when he received the Ten Commandments. On Horeb, Elijah heard God's instructions after his showdown at Mount Carmel. For the Israelites, *Horeb* was a steady reminder that their God loved to speak.

As Malachi evoked Horeb memories, he raised their expectations (perhaps unknowingly) that they would continue to find God operating in such ways. They could not have known that they would soon be disappointed. We know little of the Israelite experience between the close of Malachi and the opening words of the Gospels. The decades stretched on. People lived and died. Children were born. Dreams were dashed. Crops were harvested. Hardships and tragedies ensued. And through it all, God was silent.

Little of modern Christian teaching prepares us for the God who doesn't talk. This is odd, as much of the experience of the faithful throughout history has been in times that could properly be described as in-between. While God has appeared at dramatic moments in the developing narrative of his people, this is not the norm. Most of the Christian experience is everyday fare—humdrum, regular, some might say boring. It is living and loving, raising a family, pursuing integrity, retelling the stories of the faith, and at times wondering why it has been so long since anyone has actually *seen*, actually *heard* God.

It is no wonder these routine years get little press. There simply isn't much to write about. A giant receiving a lethal blow from the slingshot of a pesky kid, a dead man who should be rotting walking out of his tomb—these are stories that grab attention. But in the normal, banal substance of the commonplace life—sleeping and eating and wondering and dying—there just isn't much glitz. So when we face the dullness of our own lives, we may think something is wrong. It isn't. We just happen to live in a time when God has seemingly gone silent.

If this is true, it would make sense for the church to offer more tutoring for the realities one will encounter living in a time when God is essentially silent. One practice of the church offers such an education. The season of Lent is instructive for these long periods when it appears God has abandoned his post. Lent is a discipline in the mundane, an embracing of the silence and the sorrow.

The Lenten season is a dark forty-day span. Inaugurated with Ash Wednesday, it is a time for repentance, a time for sorrow, a time to sit in the void.[6] It is also a time given for preparing one's soul for Easter. Some prepare for baptism. Some renew their commitment to be disciples of Jesus. Most, if not all, grapple with the gravity of their sin. For forty days, there is a sense of sadness and loss. For forty days, the faithful engage the reality that the world is not as it should be.

The length of the season is intended as an opportunity to embrace Christ's forty days in the wilderness. Christ withdrew from the crowds, pulled himself away from his disciples, and went without food for forty days. During these lonely days, Christ wrestled and fought. Both his hunger and the Cross toward which he journeyed inflicted him with pain, the sharp sting of body and soul. Yet he did not run. He did not collapse. He lived through it, accepting it for what it was and wading through to the other side.

Because Lent looks toward Easter, there is a tendency to focus on the hope of what will come instead of to live in the reality of where we are. Hope comes, to be sure, but Lent — and the experience of Christ in the wilderness — reminds us that hope comes in its time. It won't be rushed.

A friend of mine, an Anglican priest, recently shared his frustration with the way many people in the low-church tradition (like me) treat the church's holy days as if they are commodities. It is en vogue for a church to mix the old and the new, the traditional and the edgy, the bourgeois and the bohemian. But there is a risk in this of reducing the ancient disciplines to nothing more than wares — nothing more than currency in the high-stakes game of grabbing religious market share.

The day my friend and I talked happened to be during the week of Ash Wednesday. He recounted how another pastor had told him they were going to have an Ash Wednesday service for the first time. It seemed like a good thing to do, the other pastor said. "But," this pastor added, "we are trying to lighten it up. It can be a little too somber."

"*Too* somber?" My friend didn't hide his incredulity very well. "It's one day out of 365," he continued. "Can't we mourn our sin for just one day?"

The tendency to look past Lent might appear healthy, a plausible means of dealing with the harshness of human suffering. However, a failure to give space to these bleak and afflicted portions of our lives results in our dispensing great damage on our souls. To refuse Lent is to live in denial, to insist that the world be what it isn't. It acts as though we still live in the Garden and the rebellion of Adam and Eve never happened. To refuse Lent is to live a lie.

However, to embrace Lent—honestly, if not joyfully—is to live with a profound yet holy sadness. It is to acknowledge that the Fall was tragic and that our selfish attempts to rebound from humanity's deepest calamity are sinful and destructive. To live in Lent is to have integrity, to want what is true more than what is comfortable. Lent reminds us there is such a thing as sin, try as we might to ignore it. Lent will not allow us to get away with our maneuvering or our well-planned escape from reality. Lent forces us to deal with life as it is on its own terms.

Brook Meyers said it well:

> *Much of our faith focuses on hope and possibility, as well it might. But during Lent we are given permission to banish Pollyanna for a season and acknowledge the pain and brokenness of our lives and our world. This darkening season shines a light on the fact that all is not well in Denmark, or anyplace else. It is bracingly direct and unapologetic about this hard truth. Lent keeps us from indulging in denial, from wanting to believe that God makes all things sweetness and light for the faithful, from thinking that all should be well all the time.*[7]

Without Lent, Resurrection Sunday loses its force. If there is no sin, there is no need for grace. If there is no pain, there is no need for healing. If there is no Fall, redemption has no place. Meyers goes on, "Lent allows us to embrace darkness, not as an indication of God's absence or disinterest or impotence, but as part and parcel of the lives we lead — lives shot through with grace, lives for which Jesus embraced and overcame darkness."[8]

Because there is Lent, there is a Cross, a Resurrection, a Christ. Lent, the prototype for all human in-betweenness, teaches us to honor God's silence.

The truth is that God communicates even when he doesn't speak. His voice might echo in a friendship or a child's laugh. His presence might be felt watching the sun struggle to pull itself over the darkened ridge of the Rocky Mountains.

I have a friend named Tom. He is an artist, a musician, an old soul. He tours in a beat-up blue Chevy van that blows black smoke and has a New York license plate, even though he lives in Nashville. Whenever he passes our way, we do our best to see that he spends at least a few hours in our home. We usually share a meal, but what normally passes between us is more nourishing than food. He is one of those people who says much by saying little.

When Tom came into town recently, I told him I wanted to chat. "I've had some dark days recently," I said.

"Me too," he said. Then he just stood there.

He looked at me, offering nothing but his steady presence, firm and engaged. A moment like this is often awkward. The silence is thick. Stomachs churn. Eyes are suddenly slaves to gravity, pulled to the ground or perhaps to the side — anywhere away from the steady gaze making us feel naked, exposed. This time it wasn't too awkward, though. I felt warm, as though I had been heard.

The next day Tom came to the house for lunch. We sat around the table, and I recounted some of my mental turmoil.

"Sometimes I wonder if I really believe this whole God thing," I said.

"Me too." There it was again.

"It's a scary thing to wonder if God is real or if it's all just a hoax."

"Yeah, I know."

I kept fishing for a fuller response. "It would be a bummer to find out that humanity had just invented this notion of God to deal with all the chaos in our world."

"It sure would," he replied, oblivious to my bait.

"I mean, where is God? It seems like I haven't heard him clearly in years."

Tom was warming up. "Yeah, lately I've felt really pissed off. Just last night, I was thinking God seems more moved by obedience than tears. He seems a lot more ruthless to me than he used to."

Great. I hadn't thought of that. I continued, "You know, I've had lots of doubts in my life, but this one is the trump card. This is the ultimate question, and the stakes couldn't be higher. Either God is a figment of my imagination, an empty ideal, or there is a Creator God who entered human history in the person of Jesus. It's all or nothing, and everything for me hangs in the balance."

"There are other gradients, you know. What if there is a God, but he just doesn't care?"

Well, fantastic. Let me handle my existential crisis, and then I'll just hop on over to Tom's.

Our conversation went on pretty much like that for the rest of our time together. Lots of questions, few answers. But somehow amid our words and wrestling, I felt something stir in my heart. I felt pulled toward God. Tom shared his own stories of darkness and disillusionment. He shared how he has faced his sin of arrogance and withdrawal from community. I shared how I have been confronted with my pride, convicted to repent of rejecting simplicity and making my mind an idol.

Somehow in our honest confession of doubt and faith, we were embracing each other. In that embrace, I felt God. It was short. Even as I type, I am struggling to remember the warmth of the moment. Yet it happened. I was there, and so was God.

As Tom walked out our front door that afternoon, he stepped off the porch and turned to say good-bye. His beat-up van sat in our driveway, ready to carry him to the next town, his next show. I sat at the edge of our door as he stood on our sidewalk. There we were again in that not-so-awkward stare.

"We believe in you, Tom," I said.

He stood and soaked it in. Grace rested in his eyes. "I believe in you guys too."

He drove away, and I knew I had encountered a friend. In those moments, I had experienced God. Even in the midst of silence and through another pilgrim, God made himself known. It was a conversation without words. It is uncanny how God can speak without interrupting the silence.

After Mother Teresa's death, researchers found eight volumes of documents offering rare insight into her long life of humble service to the destitute. Among those volumes were a number of personal letters revealing a vulnerable side to Mother Teresa that few knew existed.

Mother Teresa's life took an abrupt and momentous turn on September 10, 1946, as she sat in the coach of a passenger train on her way to a spiritual retreat. Rumbling along the tracks, she received a dramatic call from God. She distinctly heard God's voice. It was an inner voice, but its volume was deafening. Those who have read her accounts of the experience define the encounter as "intense" and "ecstatic." For her, a hand dropping out of the sky to carve a message on the wall would have been no clearer. God told her to create a ministry to the poorest of Calcutta.

For months after this vivid train ride, God continued to speak. Her life was a whirlwind, and her spiritual awareness bristled. God seemed to be everywhere, and she had never felt so spiritually alive.

However, things quickly changed. At just the time when one would expect God to intensify his communication — when the difficult work in Calcutta began — the "union with Jesus," as she called it, "disappeared." Her raw, emotive letters spill her disappointment, an acute anguish that would later turn to prolonged despair.

Mother Teresa lamented how God had abandoned her. She felt she had been "thrown away by God." Her journals bleed with the remorse of love lost. "I call. I cling. I want. And there is no one to answer. The darkness is so dark, and I am alone."

Her gloom pulled her into even more distressing questions about God. Fear and sorrow accompanied her as she wrote of "the terrible pain of loss, of God not wanting me, of God not being God, of God not really existing." The darkness inflicted its ultimate toll. She wondered if there really was a God at all.

On one occasion, a priest went to speak with Mother Teresa because he was looking for spiritual direction and some solace or guidance for his own distraught heart. He told her how God seemed to have abandoned him and he didn't know what to do.

"How long has it been since you have experienced in an emotional way this union with Christ?" she probed.

"Seven years."

"Well, with me it has been almost thirty."

Even at the end of her life, the darkness had not abated. Spanning almost fifty years from that distant day on the train, God's silence had been constant. Yet in her final journals, Mother Teresa penned a remarkable discovery. She had come to believe that it was in her spiritual distance from God that she was able to identify with "Christ's abandonment on the cross." Even in the silence, God was speaking.[9]

There are some things you can grasp only in silence. Some truths can be experienced only in between.

I am beginning to think part of the reason God is so often silent with us is because he wants to show us a better way. He invites us to follow his example. Uncomfortable as the silence, especially God's silence, is, it is mandatory for the Christian pilgrimage. Jesus required the wilderness and the garden — periods of grave silence, deep sorrow, and utter aloneness — to clearly hear the Father.

There are times when fierce courage demands that I speak. There are other times, however, when tenacious humility requires that I be silent. It is an act of great discipline to resist answering for God, to simply let his silence be. If he is not speaking, I do not need to fill in the awkward space in his place.

I first heard of Tom — my guitarist friend with the Chevy van and the New York plates — when we moved to Clemson, South Carolina. He is a legend there. His name would regularly come up in conversation, and I would ask, "So when is he coming back?"

"We don't know. He isn't singing right now."

Apparently, Tom was a silent singer.

As I grew to know Tom and heard more of his story, I found out that he needed time away for solitude and rest, a season away from the road and the crowd and all the noise. I respect his courage to step away, to refuse to offer what everyone expects of him. It is a courage of silence.

Why is it so unusual for me to be silent, to push pause on the relentless activity? Why must I always have something to say? Why must I always attempt to explain God's mysteries or offer a swift summary response to even the most reflective questions?[10] God suffers from none of these obsessions.

I am afraid of the quiet. In the quiet, my snarling doubts might overwhelm me. For me to be silent, I must be broken. I fear that my addiction to chatter, my eagerness to always have a prompt reply, hints that I am unwilling to face the plainest truth: I live in a world that isn't heaven. God invites me to hear the hollow echo of nothingness, to feel the cold, biting reality of dreams coming to naught. His invitation comes wrapped in silence. Without a sound, his charge to me is to own up to my brokenness and in so doing find grace.

Tom eventually emerged from the solitude and once again began to share the gift of his music. His first recording after his hiatus was simple, bare. Titled *Country Dog, City Boy* (who wouldn't love an album with that name?), it offered simply Tom, his guitar and pungent lyrics alive and fresh. On the dustcover, he reflects on the past year's journey: "After a year of 'laying low' it's good to be playing music again, though

I'm learning that all of it, especially the silence, is a song."[11] Like Tom, I am learning that silence can sing. Silence can scream.

Oswald Chambers was fond of saying that silence is required in order to hear God speak. He suggested that it is only when we are despondent, alone, and utterly ruined by the disappointments of all we thought or knew we had going in our favor that silence can find its place with us.

When silence does find its place, when it snuggles in for a long winter's stay, it begins its work. It burrows past our defenses and tears apart our well-oiled mechanisms for coping with the worst life offers. We become defenseless, vulnerable to the ravages of all we have worked so hard to deny. It undoes us, leaving us nothing. And, as Chambers would say, when all that is left for us is the ghostly silence, then, maybe then, we might be in a place humble enough to actually listen.

CHAPTER 10

of God and fireflies

What we hunger for most, we worship.

—JOHN PIPER

You are chosen, you resist, you resort to rage and bitterness and, finally, you succumb to the God who has given you your identity in the first place.

—KATHLEEN NORRIS

"They may build, but I will demolish. . . . You will see it with your own eyes and say, 'Great is the LORD — even beyond the borders of Israel!'"

—MALACHI 1:4-5

Summers in Tennessee were a young, adventurous boy's dream. I grew up on a ranch with horses grazing in our backyard and real live cowboys as neighbors. With over six thousand acres to roam, imaginary battles and heroic fantasies had plenty of space. My best friend lived next door, and together we explored as many of these acres as we could. Lookout Mountain was our favorite hike. Packing a lunch and a Lone Ranger six-shooter, we would set off for the top of the world.

Evenings also held a unique enchantment. Around dusk—after supper but before our moms would call us in for the baths we insisted we didn't need—we would grab Mason jars and hunt those elusive and tempting shimmers of light, fireflies. Hundreds of fireflies would pulse across our front yards, providing us a gallery of shooting stars and small flickering bursts of light.

I don't know why fireflies fascinated us so much. Perhaps it was the magical flicker and glow as their illumined tails flashed against the encroaching twilight. Perhaps we believed we were chasing after fairies or Peter Pan's Tinkerbell. The fireflies were strange and mysterious. *How do they light up? What makes them spark? If we captured enough, could they light up our bedrooms all night long?*

We would chase and run and laugh, grabbing as many fireflies as we could catch. As the night settled and my mom called my name, I would take my jar inside, put aluminum foil across the top, and poke a few holes to let in air. I would set it on the windowsill and drift off to sleep, weary and worn yet pleased that I had captured a bit of the mystery. The wild and flashing fireflies I had caught were a bit tamer now, a little less mystifying, a little less alluring. They were in a jar, and their light dimly blushed against the cool glass.

There is something inbred into the human spirit that drives us toward conquest. We like to control. Social criticism has long warned us against the vices of our extreme consumerist culture. Under the guise of human progress, some of our most cherished resources are being discarded. Natural beauty is surrendered on the altar of suburban sprawl. Human contact is gobbled up by sterile technological communication.

Architecture and the arts are forced into submission by the crippling demand of function over form. Our pragmatism might appear to offer certain improvements, but the price paid for this forward movement is costly. With such conquering advancements, something is lost — a bit of beauty, a bit of who we are. And we forget that humans are not ultimate. There is something — Someone — more.

Yet control we must. There is no place for ambiguity. If there is a question, we will scratch at it until we have found an answer or there is nothing left for us to query. If there is uncertainty, we will poke and prod until we feel confident and safe, knowing all there is to know and leaving nothing unexplored. If anything is unknown or untamed, inexplicable or subtle or bewildering, it is unacceptable. It must be dismantled or defined. It must be explained or discounted. Mystery simply will not do.

So we dissect it with our logic. We bludgeon it with our unyielding demands that it fit into our system or conform to our paradigms. If it doesn't, it will be dismissed. Anything that stretches outside our parameters or refuses to be pushed into the mold will be trimmed off and discarded. It's safer that way.

We grab what we can, and we stuff it into a jar. We rest easy as the tamed mystery flickers in its proper place, barricaded by aluminum foil and enclosed in glass.

On the mornings after my firefly hunts, I would wake to a disappointing sight. The fanciful, glowing insects danced no more. Instead, they lay wilted and crumpled at the bottom of the jar, their light gone. Fireflies cannot live in captivity and are unable to adapt to closed spaces.

True mystery cannot be contained. I try such antics with God. I demand he conform to my sense of precision. I insist he tell me what he will *always* do and how he will *always* respond. I convince myself I can determine most of his patterns and assumptions and veins of thought. These antics are subtle but sick. And they are hopelessly misguided.

It has been an arduous, grinding road. There have been moments when I thought I had him under control, but he always slips away. My attempts to cast a theological net over God always fall short, and my attempts to force him into a corner with intense intellectual rigor never pan out. I have been hell-bent on stuffing him into my Mason jar, but he just won't cooperate.

And he never will. God can never be captured. He can never be reduced or dissected. His glory exudes otherness, and to know him, to truly know him, we will simply have to step into his other world. He refuses to be confined to ours — it is far too small.

The message of Malachi with all of its strangeness and harsh boldness is primarily a call to worship. The prophet's message is startling because it runs counter to the core human sin: the exaltation of self. The act of worship is ultimate humility. It is the moment when we take our expectations, our requirements, and our idolatrous self-interest and modestly lay them down before the One who makes all these things appear so petty and slight.

The things we control, the things we can easily manage, do not evoke our awe. They do not arrest our passions or melt our delusions of self-grandeur. If we can harness them and hustle the manpower to hold on to the reins, then we are in charge. We are bigger. We might as well continue our indulgent love. We might as well worship ourselves.

This is why Malachi speaks disorienting words, words that shock and baffle. This is why Malachi perplexes and confounds. He is speaking of God. And to a people deluded by the arrogant belief that they are in charge, that they are forefront, God offers the definitive disorientation.

Malachi reminds Israel of their God who is bold and in charge and can never be dumbed down by pithy little propositions or tidily hemmed in by trite theological jargon. Malachi will not allow the people to rest in their self-deception. He will not leave them to the inevitable destruction that comes from the illusory view of a small God and a large self.

He disrupts their ease by dismantling their construction of a quaint God who can be easily managed, who hopes for little and requires even less. He charges through a litany of bewildering realities. God will hate Esau if he so chooses. God will curse and ravage when he deems it necessary. God will answer prayers — or not — at the time he considers appropriate. God will entice with beauty and bless with silence. God will, at times, allow the wicked to seemingly go unpunished while the righteous writhe in despair. He will not be robbed. He will not be coerced. He will do what he will do. When he chooses. How he chooses. He is God.

And when the people are bewildered by this abrupt and looming God-reality, the response is at it should be: worship.

The monastery of Saint John's Abbey provided Kathleen Norris solace and an immersion in spiritual reflection. During one of her stays, she participated in the practice of *lectio continua* in which the monks read through entire books of the Bible, small portions at a time, throughout a sequence of morning and evening prayers.

They had recently begun reading Jeremiah, and the monks and novices were realizing how long it was going to take them to make their way through this thick book. She remembers one monk expressing his appreciation that on this cycle, Jeremiah was being read during morning prayers rather than evening when guests were more apt to be present. "The monks can take it," he said, "but most people have no idea what's in the Bible, and they come unglued."[1]

The monk could have been speaking of our encounter with Malachi. The prophet arrests our attention and disorients our equilibrium, and if we allow this discomfort to do its work, we worship. *Worship* is simply another way of expressing how we come unglued.

Isaiah 24:1 echoes a similar theme:

> *See, the LORD is going to lay waste the earth*
> *and devastate it;*
> *he will ruin its face*
> *and scatter its inhabitants.*

It's difficult to imagine much harsher words. Definitely not a Hallmark moment. So what is the response of the people?

> *They raise their voices, they shout for joy;*
> *from the west they acclaim the LORD's majesty.*
> *Therefore in the east give glory to the LORD."*[2]

God ravages, and the people worship. There are moments when God breaches our defenses and we find there is something we want more than safety: God. Worship brims when our hearts are captured by something bigger than we are. And sincere God-enflamed worship is what we were created for. It is our truest pleasure.

This is why God refuses our silly attempts to confine and corner him. He desires our worship, and he has created us for ultimate ecstasy. He has breathed into our souls a craving for the sort of delight that will be realized only in the utterly uninhibited immersion in the one thing that can satiate our unrelenting yearning for the Divine. This one thing, God knows, is himself.[3]

And so for the sake of his ultimate glory (which he will jealously guard and will never yield) and for our ultimate pleasure, God remains outside our bounds. He breaks our perceptions and disappoints our expectations. He knows we will never worship, will never love, will never receive soul-deep pleasure from any object we control.

This is why God will unleash savage grace or go silent or speak from places and voices we never would have expected. God is God, and he has the clearest sense of what must be done and spoken, our expectations aside.

It had been a month since my engagement to Miska turned sour, and I was a real mess. The setting had been perfect. Miska and I were on top of Keystone Mountain overlooking Summit County, Colorado, and its rugged peaks. It was an early January evening with stars strung out across the sky and the brisk air forming to our breath. I dropped down on one knee and asked the most beautiful woman I have ever known to marry me. Amazingly, she said yes.

But something went awry between that romantic moment and our arrival back home in Texas. I freaked out. The drive back home was long, the many miles filled with painful talks and lots of silence. Before the trip ended, I had a diamond ring back in my pocket.

After I returned from the Colorado fiasco, I sat in my previously scheduled appointment with a psychiatrist who had been helping me struggle through another issue. On this particular day, he spoke out of turn. He meddled. Leaning back in his chair, he offered bluntly, "Winn, it's time for you to be a man. You need to make up your mind about Miska, and then you need to buck up and do it. No more whining."

Is this a typical psychiatric method? Beyond the fact that this particular issue was none of his concern, I expected a little more compassion, a little more introspection into the deep-seated roots of my anguish. Perhaps I would lie on the couch with dimmed lights and soft acoustic music. We would probe into my hurts and maybe even blame this unfortunate situation on my parents.

But he had told me to buck up, to stop whining. He had called me out, refused me an exit. He offered a savage grace.

God is busy calling me out, refusing me an exit. He offers grace that at the time seems like everything but. He speaks when I expect a little solitude, and he goes mute when I expect communication to be fast and free. Frankly, there are many times when I just can't make sense of him. *What is he up to? What is he doing? Is he doing anything?*

God is near. He is personal. The Incarnation demonstrated God's identity with broken humanity. His humiliation on the cross and his victory in the Resurrection forever secured a radical embracing of his sinful and rebellious creation. Yet the otherness of God is a reality we will never escape. Try as we might, God will always be shrouded in some form of mystery. It must be so or the creature is equal to the Creator. Mystery is not something to be scorned or avoided. It is to be embraced. It is part of the wonder of the awesome moment when the human is in the presence of the Almighty.

The danger of exploring mysteries, even as we give a nod to its proper place in our experience, is that somehow we begin to sense that through the exploring, we are grabbing a little more of a handle on these shadow realities. Mystery, contradictorily, becomes more familiar. We get comfortable with the idea.

And then God makes another unexpected turn.

As I explore this terrain, it has been tempting to believe that I am finding a groove, that by continually maintaining the presence of the questions, they somehow become easier, less uncomfortable. Perhaps my talk of mystery is just another way of giving it a trim, of trying to corner its unruly edges so I can feel as if I have it under some semblance of control.

And then God makes another unexpected turn.

As I write, I sit in a beautiful, small English-styled chapel. Framed with stone and timber, the chapel is nestled on top of Glassy Mountain on the edge of a sheer rock cliff dropping several hundred feet. The view stretches for miles. Inside the chapel, the wooden pews face south toward the front where the pastor would stand, and huge windows display the vivid image of sky and distant mountains. It is breathtaking.

Today, however, the clouds hover right at the edge of the cliff. It seems I could just stretch my hand and grab a wisp of fluffy whiteness. There is a haze below the clouds, giving the space an eerie, almost gloomy tint. When I look down the drop below the haze, I can still make out the lower hills. I see houses and a few roads. In the distance, I can just barely make out the shores of a lake.

Yet the clouds are closing in. They control my vision. They will allow me to see what they deem fitting. With a steady and unflustered control, they have settled in. They are in charge, and all I can do is yield to their force.

My God-questions have not grown fewer. My sense of frustration with his unconformity has not lessened. I am finding that he has simply settled in. He is in charge, and all I can do is yield to his force.

Several months ago, I was feeling dark despair. Several spiritual questions plagued my mind, and the grip of doubt was unrelenting. I was back to the questions of God's reality. It was heavy and brutal. To make matters worse, I had endured a conflict with a friend whom I had poured much of my life into. This friend appeared to be siding with someone who had issues with me. I felt betrayed and abandoned. It was not a good combination.

That weekend, I was performing a wedding. The location was an hour and a half from home, and Miska wasn't able to go with me. On the return trip, I was brooding over the betrayal I felt from my friend, and I began to play out scenarios in my mind, conversations I would like to have with the exact words I would like to say.

Don't you trust me? I would say. *I'm not asking for your blind faith,* I would add. *Don't we have a history? Even if you don't have all the facts, can't you trust my heart?*

The words still dangled when the Spirit spoke.[4] *Don't you trust me?* he said. *I'm not asking for your blind faith,* he added. *Don't we have a history? Even if you don't have all the facts, can't you trust my heart?*

I don't know that I have ever felt more repentant than at that moment. My heart had been deeply wounded by the disloyalty I felt from my friend. I didn't understand how trust could be so easily discarded. Why did my friend demand details and time lines and facts when he had seen deeper things, such as my heart and my soul, my truest essence?

I believe God feels something similar. Why do I require answers and proof and precise explanation when I have experienced mercy and beauty, grace and joy?

At some point, I must make a decision. Do I want myself, or do I want God? Will I cling to the false hope of undeniable certainty, or will I embrace all of God, the clear as well as the murky, the plain as well as the mysterious?

"Decision," Kierkegaard tells us, "is the awakening to the eternal."[5] There comes a moment, and for me it is many moments, when the frightening decision waits. Will I plunge into God, drinking in the wonder and startling veracity of One who offers me nothing other than the promise that he is God and will be my God until the very end? These points of departure are predicated on nothing more than God and his promises. Trembling and uncertain, I close my eyes, hold my nose, and dive.

And eternity happens. Worship erupts. I am helpless, hopeless even, unless God comes through. These places of abandonment are obviously foolish and insane unless God is who he says he is. And on the rare occasions when I do throw caution to the wind and leap, my heart is open, alive, bowed to my God.

Wendy Wright tells us that "our deepest intuitions, guided by the wisdom of the faith, do not turn us into ourselves but orient us toward one another, and finally, toward our end and beginning, our God."[6] Unfortunately, our deepest intuitions have been short-circuited by sin. Pride, self-protection, and fear muddle what should be clear — that we want God. But instead of being clear, this reality is distorted, and rather than desiring to commune with God, we wrangle to control him. And we try to bottle him up like a firefly.

Thankfully, he does not cooperate. With a mysterious voice, he speaks to our deepest longings, past the sin and the haze, and tells us once again that he is God.

As I have journeyed toward God on this path of mystery, the kind of clarity I have sought has been entirely elusive. There are many good days, days of light and hope and peace. I cherish these, but I am learning to hold them loosely, to see them as a gift. There are also many gloomy days, days of questions and obsessions and thoughts that spiral ever inward, ever darker. I often feel trapped, cornered by my precarious predicament of uncertainty and restlessness.

Last Sunday a guy asked how I was doing. When I am in difficult seasons, I loathe the question. I don't want to give a dishonest, pious response, but I grow weary of sounding ominous and doomful. I want to say something bright, something that fits well in a jocular cartoon with strange animals that talk in funny voices or is reminiscent of one of those cheery detergent commercials expounding how the world is changed because grass stains have finally been tamed.

Unfortunately, no cartoon voices came to mind. "The past two weeks have been tough," I answered. And they have been.

But not today. Today I feel hope. Today I feel life. It is not that I have found some final resolution. Questions remain, and God still resists bending toward my whims. The difference is that God has reminded me who he is — God. I have repented, again, of my urge to usurp his place. For today, I have found serenity in abandoning myself to the chaos rather than trying to manage it. For today, I have surrendered my spiritual disarray at the feet of my God, and I am free to worship, free to dance. I am not God, and a load is lifted.

When I take on the weight of trying to figure God out, believing that in capturing him I can minimize my emotional risk and protect the life I hold dear, I take a step into death — cold, miserable, self-absorbed death. Paul reminds me that "obsession with self in these matters is a dead end; attention to God leads us out into the open, into a spacious, free life."[7] This spacious, free life is what I want. More than I want to know and more than I want to manage or control, I want a heart that is open, willing to risk, willing to abandon for the sake of love, willing to run into the dangerous worship of a God outside my bounds. And so I dash into the spaciousness of God.

I can't know what tomorrow will bring. But today I am dancing in the chaos. I am waltzing in the mystery.

reader's guide

Use these questions to delve deep into the intersection of your story and God's mystery. Wrestle with them on your own or consider using them as a diving board into small-group discussion.

PROLOGUE: CONFESSIONS OF A PILGRIM

1. How do the early years of your life story compare to Winn's? Were you raised in a Christian home? How did that inform your choices and lifestyle?

2. What are your initial thoughts about this quote: "Human experience tells us that nothing we most deeply value — friendships, marriage, children — surrenders to the demands for certainty"?

3. In what ways do you live with the fear that your hopes will be dashed? What drives those fears?

4. Is it easy or difficult for you to plunge into mystery, into uncertainty? Why?

5. What are your initial impressions of the book of Malachi? What restlessness do you uncover in the story presented there?

CHAPTER 1: SAVAGE GRACE

1. Do you default to a picture of God as a God of love, or is your first thought about God something different? Why do you think this is?

2. What is your reaction to the idea that God's "ferocious words" in Malachi 1:2-3 — "turned his mountains into a wasteland and left his inheritance to the desert jackals" — are given as proof of his love?

3.. Think of examples in today's society in which people have "nudged God from his center place." What leads people to discard God?

4. Are you more like Winn's son Wyatt, who is "enamored with creation," or Winn himself, who doesn't hear God's whispered words of romance? Why do you think you're like that?

5. What does "harsh love" look like to you in your circumstances? How do you respond to it?

CHAPTER 2: THE DARKER SIDE OF FAITH

1. Have you ever prayed with as much certainty as the student who prayed that a likely rainstorm would not come? When did you do that? What were the results?

2. Think of a circumstance when you prayed, hoped, and were disappointed. To what did/do you attribute the apparent silence of God or the answer that wasn't what you'd hoped for?

3. Have you ever used your faith as a means to "make God move" or to get what you want? What did that look like?

4. If you can recall a time when "God didn't come through" for you, describe that circumstance. What were your feelings toward God? How did you reconcile the situation (if you have)?

5. Respond to this quote: "God seems to do whatever he pleases with little regard for my schemes, and that is utterly disconcerting."

CHAPTER 3: STEPPING INTO THE STORY

1. What are your immediate responses to Winn's description of the unease in his soul as he preaches? Do you imagine this is true for the pastor who preaches at your church? Why or why not?

2. Read this excerpt: "When we gather as God's people each and every Sunday, we are participating in the ancient practice of remembering, retelling, and embracing the story of God and his dealings with his people." How is this like or unlike your church experience?

3. In what ways do you enter "God's narrative" during the week? Does this happen at church? At home? Elsewhere? Describe these times.

4. Do you agree or disagree with this statement: "To forget the form of story, to not allow it center stage, is to miss God." Explain your answer.

5. What is your reaction to the proposition that "we can't control the stories. They control us"? Is it easy for you to step into the "wild and mysterious narrative"? Why or why not?

CHAPTER 4: RISK OF DOUBT

1. Okay, be honest. What was your initial reaction to the first sentence in this chapter? What did you expect to discover as you read further? Were your expectations confirmed?

2. Describe the time or times of significant doubt in your life. What preceded those seasons? Are you in one now? How do you move through them?

3. Think of something that doubt stole from your life. What was it like to work through that? Can you recapture what was lost? How?

4. Respond to this excerpt: "As I now see it, faith and doubt are bedfellows — strange ones, indeed, but partners all the same. Faith requires, to at least some degree, some possibility that I could be wrong."

5. What is your reaction to this quote: "If God is daring and bold and free, if God skirts the wild edges, then following him means we will make friends with hazard and peril"? Do you think God "skirts the wild edges"? What does that look like in your experience of him?

CHAPTER 5: TWILIGHT KNOWING

1. What are some ways you've investigated your faith? What did you discover in the process?

2. How do you explain those "things you just know" in life? How is this similar to or different from the "twilight knowing" Winn talks about?

3. What are your reactions to this statement: "It would seem that however diligently we might try, we can't conclusively separate knowledge, whether scientific or spiritual, from some manner of faith"?

4. Do you believe we can find pleasure "apart from God"? Why or why not?

5. In what ways do you try to control God? What prompts that way of thinking? How is giving up that control a way of entering the "twilight knowing"?

CHAPTER 6: SEX AND SACRAMENT

1. This might be a difficult chapter for you to explore for many reasons. Begin by sharing your initial thoughts about this topic as candidly as you are able.

2. What is your reaction to God's "abrupt declaration" that something was "not good" in creation prior to his creation of woman? What does this suggest to you about the value of human-to-human relationships? About marriage? About sex?

3. Paul describes the concept of "one flesh" in marriage as a profound mystery. Why do you think Paul compares this union to the example of Christ and the church? Does that bother you? Confuse you? Confirm something you already believe?

4. Offer your reactions and thoughts about this statement: "Nakedness, the fully exposed human body, is a treacherous power."

5. Winn speaks to the intent of sex, to the ideal. In light of that, what is your response to the following excerpt: "Sex is not primarily urges or arousals. It is not technique, and it is not ultimately defined by orgasm. Sex is a mysterious act of worship that whispers something of God to us."

CHAPTER 7: THE DEEP WATERS OF LAMENT

1. What stories or statements in Scripture most unnerve you? How do you respond to the more brutal chapters in God's story?

2. Read this statement: "When faith is separated from its opportunity to connect with and emerge from the grieving, sorrowful, desolate places of the soul, our spiritual experience owns the proper words but misses much of the heart." What does this mean in practical terms? Can you relate it to your own life? Explain.

3. How do you think you'd respond if your pastor spoke directly to the congregation as David spoke to God in one of his brazen rants? What does this say about our ability to handle the difficult truths of Scripture? What does it say about the church?

4. Do you find it easy, difficult, or impossible to lament? Why do you think you respond that way?

5. Describe the difference between biblical lament and disconnecting with God. Can you recall times when you've experienced both? What was the result of each of those experiences?

CHAPTER 8: WHISPER OF PLEASURE

1. Does God laugh? Explain why you think he does or doesn't. Why is it important to wrestle with this question?

2. How do you react to the discussion of pleasure in this chapter? Does it come naturally for you to talk about pleasure in the context of your faith life? Why do you think that is?

3. Read the Creation story in Genesis. Do you see the pleasure in this story that Winn writes about? Where else do you see evidence of God's pleasure?

4. React to this definition of pleasure: "Giving occasion and space and respect to what is most alive in us, to that surge that reminds us we aren't yet dead."

5. What does it mean that we are "crafted for delight"? Do you agree with that? What is the greatest challenge in living out God-saturated pleasure?

CHAPTER 9: BETWEEN

1. As you look at the larger faith story in which you play a part, what clues tell you this is an in-between time? How does that make you feel?

2. How do you react to times when God seems silent in your life?

3. Think about the ways you celebrate (or don't celebrate) the season of Lent. Is there anything in this chapter that prompts you to reconsider how you approach this season?

4. Respond to this statement: "Lent, the prototype for all human in-betweenness, teaches us to honor God's silence."

5. What lessons has God's silence taught you? What do you long for God to say to break the silence?

Chapter 10: Of God and Fireflies

1. Think about your drive toward conquest. How does that play out in your everyday existence? In your relationship with God?

2. "God can never be captured." What does the truth of this statement do to your faith? How does it inform the manner in which you try to grow closer to God?

3. Respond to this statement: "The danger of exploring mysteries, even as we give a nod to its proper place in our experience, is that somehow we begin to sense that through the exploring, we are grabbing a little more of a handle on these shadow realities." Is this true of your experience as you read this book? Explain.

4. Describe a time when you closed your eyes and dove into the mystery of God. In what ways was that a worship experience?

5. If you desire to "dance in the chaos," what would it take to do so? Is this something you can do all the time? In seasons? What role does God play in that process?

notes

PROLOGUE: CONFESSIONS OF A PILGRIM

1. Stanley J. Grenz, *A Primer on Postmodernism* (Grand Rapids, MI: Eerdmans, 1996), 81.
2. Jonathan Edwards, quoted in Stephen J. Nichols, "The Mind Shapers," *Christian History* 22, no. 1: 22.
3. Eugene H. Peterson, *A Long Obedience in the Same Direction*, 2nd ed. (Downers Grove, IL: InterVarsity, 2000), 45. This classic work on Christian discipleship grazes through the fifteen Songs of Ascents (see Psalms 120–134) to offer an honest, thoroughly inviting though refreshingly unspectacular understanding of the path of following God for a lifetime. Quick steps and guaranteed processes are in short supply here, and this biblical integrity is what endears many to Peterson's spiritual guidance.

CHAPTER 1: SAVAGE GRACE

1. Deuteronomy 20:16-18, Joshua 6:15-21, and 1 Samuel 15 are a few of the more difficult passages to read.
2. This disturbing conflict, pitting the picture of a kind and gracious God against a harsh and vengeful God, has been the subject of much theological inquiry. An extreme answer has been to propose a two-God motif, a raging God of the Hebrew Bible (where the majority of the harsher stories are found) and a loving God of the New Testament (where God's gracious nature is more fully explored). Orthodoxy has soundly withstood this venture. A more commonly accepted proposal has been to chalk the conflict up to a difference in *how God works* rather than *who God is*. This attempt centers on deciphering God's economy (ways of dealing with humans) between law and grace. While there is something to be said for distinctions under the

Old Covenant and the New, the problem is not resolved so neatly. Obviously, Ananias and Sapphira were under the New Covenant, as were the Corinthians who were soundly warned of God's judgment. Further, while not revealed as fully, grace was certainly abundant in the Old Covenant.

3. C. S. Lewis, *The Chronicles of Narnia: The Lion, the Witch and the Wardrobe* (New York: Harper Collins, 1994), 85–86.

4. Peter Verhoef notes that the Hebrew text goes out of its way to affirm their brotherhood, as if it were key to the prophet's assertion. His literal rendering of this line in Malachi 1:2 is, "Was he not a brother, viz., Esau of Jacob?" Peter Verhoef, *The New International Commentary on the Old Testament: The Books of Haggai and Malachi* (Grand Rapids, MI: Eerdmans, 1987), 199.

5. Malachi 1:2-3.

6. Persian rule allowed a good deal of autonomy for Israel, something denied with the more stringent governorship of previous occupations. They were allowed to have some determination over their own borders, to interact politically within the Persian system, and even to raise up their own military for certain purposes. While certainly not free, this scenario allowed as much latitude as Israel would ever know under foreign rule. See Andrew E. Hill, *The Anchor Bible: Malachi* (New York: Doubleday, 1998), 57–66.

7. The precise words were, "How have you loved us?" (Malachi 1:2).

8. Malachi 2:2-5, emphasis added.

9. There were precise regulations for discarding the sacrificial waste: either burning it in a delicate manner or burying it outside the camp. So "there's a certain irony in the prophet's condemnation, in that the priests have shown decorous sensitivity in the handling of offal from the animal sacrifices but have failed to accord equal respect to Yahweh himself." See Hill, 201.

10. Aron's story can be found in his autobiographical work *Between a Rock and a Hard Place* (New York: Atria, 2004).

11. Obadiah 1:10.

CHAPTER 2: THE DARKER SIDE OF FAITH

1. C. S. Lewis, *A Grief Observed* (Greenwich, CT: The Leabury Press, 1961), 9. Lewis published this under the pseudonym N. W. Clerk purportedly, at least in part, to limit the unsettling correspondence he would receive from those he wanted to help but would not have the energy to give personal attention to.

2. Malachi 2:17, my paraphrase. The actual question posed by the people is one taut with sarcasm.

3. Such thinking has been popularly critiqued as self-actualizing theology. However, this has most often been directed toward only the extreme and unsophisticated versions. A broader, more acceptable version of faith's insisting on certainty while giving little room for intense despair and questioning seems to be the norm.

4. A reading of Hebrews 11:32-38 can be augmented by the sober pages of *Foxe's Book of Martyrs*, which has been recently rereleased in unedited form. The testimony of the church is more of one living under the edge of the sword than one yielding cultural or political power. It is only in recent centuries in the Western world that we have grown accustomed to such a luxurious and benign atmosphere. In fact, taken to another level, Stanley Hauerwas argues in writing and lectures that American Christianity in particular faces the dire situation of embracing a social construct that is convenient to our faith but ruinous in the end. His provocatively phrased question asks, "Is America a safe place for Christianity?"

5. Crabb's book *The Pressure's Off* (WaterBrook, 2004) deals with this false ideal within the context of our commitment to living according to the Old Covenant rather than within the grace of the New Covenant.

6. Hebrews 11:39, emphasis added.

7. Hebrews 11:13, emphasis added.

8. Rabbi Harold Kushner, *When Bad Things Happen to Good People* (New York: Schocken Books, 1981), 10. Kushner wrote this book out of the context of his own struggles with the death of Aaron, his fourteen-year-old son. The book has seen more than twenty years pass since its original publication, but Kushner's brutal honesty asks many of the brooding questions that haunt us if we take God — and life — seriously.

9. Kushner, 11-12.

CHAPTER 3: STEPPING INTO THE STORY

1. William H. Willimon, *Pastor: The Theology and Practice of Ordained Ministry* (Nashville: Abingdon, 2000), 21.
2. Robert E. Webber, *Ancient-Future Time: Forming Spirituality Through the Christian Year* (Grand Rapids, MI: Baker, 2004), 152.
3. Wendy M. Wright, *Seasons of a Family's Life* (San Francisco: Jossey-Bass, 2003), 23.
4. Exodus 20:2.
5. Wright, 8.
6. Robert Benson, *Venite: A Book of Daily Prayer* (New York: Tarcher/ Putnam, 2000), 124.
7. Dr. H. Beecher Hicks Jr., "The 27th Annual State of the Church Address" (speech, Metropolitan Baptist Church, Washington, D.C., January 25, 2004).
8. This address can be found on Metropolitan's website, www.metropolitanbaptist.org/Publications/2004StateofChurch.pdf.
9. Malachi 2:10.

CHAPTER 4: RISK OF DOUBT

1. It would seem that determining whether our doubts are sinful or not should be judged with at least these criteria: (1) What is the desire of our soul — for God or for self-rule? and (2) What is the long journey of this struggle — does it ultimately lead us toward the Father or away from him?
2. Avery Cardinal Dulles, "The Rebirth of Apologetics," *First Things*, May 2004, 18.
3. Blaise Pascal, *Pensees, Section III: Of the Necessity of the Wager*, pense 229, www.classicallibrary.org/pascal/pensees/index.htm.
4. Malachi 3:10. The gambling imagery is one possible lexical flavoring.
5. See John 6:68.
6. Mel Gibson, interview by Diane Sawyer, *ABC News' Primetime Live*, ABC, February 16, 2004.

CHAPTER 5: TWILIGHT KNOWING

1. Hershel Shanks, quoted in "Contrasting Insights of Biblical Giants," *Biblical Archaeological Review*, July/August 2004, 35.
2. Kathleen Norris, *The Cloister Walk* (New York: Riverhead Books, 1996), 11.

3. R. C. Lewontin, *Biology as Ideology: The Doctrine of DNA* (New York: HarperCollins, 1991), 7.

4. Esther Lightcap Meek, *Longing to Know: The Philosophy of Knowledge for Ordinary People* (Grand Rapids, MI: Brazos Press, 2003), 65.

5. In 2003, I interviewed Yancey after the release of his book *Rumors of Another World*. His story and honest experiences struggling with God and faith are a profound encouragement to me.

6. Hosea 2:6-7 is a dramatic account of God's hemming in. He tells Hosea he will take Israel into the desert and "hedge up her way with thorns" (NASB). In love, God planned to corner, to trap those he loved, those who had abandoned him. This is another example of God's bold, fierce love.

7. Meek, 59.

8. Mevlâna Jalâluddîn Rumi, "Wean Yourself," quoted in Gordan MacKenzie, *Orbiting the Giant Hairball* (New York: Viking Press, 1998), 3.

9. I am not attempting to brush all the theological implications related to the act of Communion and baptism aside with a simplistic appeal to mystery and paradox. There are major theological divides that cannot and should not be ignored. However, it is my sense that there is also something more going on in these long-entrenched debates. Perhaps an embracing of mystery would provide a way to pursue a more fruitful discussion of our differences.

10. Leonard J. Vander Zee, *Christ, Baptism and the Lord's Supper: Recovering the Sacraments for Evangelical Worship* (Downers Grove, IL: InterVarsity, 2004), 25.

11. John Calvin, *Institutes of the Christian Religion* (4.17.32), trans. Henry Beveridge, vol. 2 (Grand Rapids, MI: Eerdmans, 1953), 587, emphasis added.

12. Peter Hiett, "Room for Doubt, Room for Faith, and Room for Me," (sermon, Lookout Mountain Community Church, Golden, CO, February 1, 2004).The sermon can be read online at http://www.lomcc.org/2004%20Sermons/02-01-04.pdf.

Chapter 6: Sex and Sacrament

1. See Ephesians 5:31-32.

2. See also Ephesians 2:1-10. Many other Pauline passages carry similar instruction. It was a standard occurrence for Paul to spend a considerable amount of time reminding the church who Christ had created it to be before he embarked on the ethical implications of these spiritual realities.

3. This is not to imply that those who are not married are of less value or participate less fully in the work of God's kingdom. On the contrary, Paul makes the case that singleness is of great value to God's purposes on the earth and is, in fact, at times to be preferred over marriage. The point I am making is that Paul seems to see the union of marriage, man and woman united, as an expression of his own reality of community.

4. Genesis 2:18.

5. Genesis 1:26, my paraphrase.

6. Genesis 1:27-28; 2:22-25.

7. This incarnational stream in Scripture is a fascinating study with numerous practical implications pertaining to God's continuing work of incarnating himself in his people, his church.

8. R. Laird Harris, ed., *Theological Wordbook of the Old Testament* (Chicago: Moody, 1980), entry 1409.

9. G. Johannes Botterweck and Helmer Ringgren, eds., *Theological Dictionary of the Old Testament*, vol. 4 (Grand Rapids, MI: Eerdmans, 1974), 83.

10. Genesis 2:25.

11. See Malachi 2:15. There is some debate about the translation and interpretation of this difficult Hebrew phrase. One option is that "one" is a reference to God the Father, alluding back to Malachi 2:10. In this understanding, the emphasis rests on the human relationship and oneness with God. I have obviously opted for a second, more supported reading that sees Malachi alluding to Genesis 2:24 with the emphasis resting on the physical and spiritual oneness God creates between a husband and a wife. In the end, however, this chapter is actually arguing for a bit of both. I do think it quite possible and fitting with both the context and biblical theology to make a case for linking the very real and sensuous oneness of man and woman to our oneness with God.

12. Malachi 2:15.

13. See Malachi 2:15. This passage is one of the most difficult to translate from the book of Malachi. My interpretation here is based on one of the well-defended views demonstrated by the translation offered in the *English Standard Version*: "Did he not make them one, with a portion of the Spirit in their union?"

14. Ephesians 5:31.

15. Ephesians 5:32.

16. Traditions unfamiliar with the term *sacrament* still reflect some similarities to sacramental practices through their "ordinances" of baptism and Communion.

17. See 2 Samuel 6:1-7.

18. Mike Mason, *The Mystery of Marriage* (Sisters, OR: Multnomah, 2001), 149. I have found few books on marriage that have captured my imagination and truly enticed me to the deep waters of marriage. Mason's *The Mystery of Marriage* is a rare exception.

19. Mason, 149.

20. I am obviously using *sacrament* in the more general sense — sex as an outworking of the more clearly established and historically held sacraments of the church.

21. Marva Dawn, *Sexual Character* (Grand Rapids, MI: Eerdmans, 1993), 18.

CHAPTER 7: THE DEEP WATERS OF LAMENT

1. Eugene Peterson, *Leap over a Wall: Earthy Spirituality for Everyday Christians* (New York: HarperSanFrancisco, 1997), 120.

2. Walter Brueggemann, *Praying the Psalms* (Winona, MN: St. Mary's Press, 1993), 17.

3. Brueggemann, 19.

4. Malachi 3:13.

5. This reality of the people's disappointment with life is one of the interpretive complexities of Malachi. In one sense, as has earlier been suggested, the Hebrew situation was a vast improvement over the long years of foreign oppression. They had more prosperity, more autonomy, and more stability under Persian rule than had been available to them for several generations. However, there were still the struggles of an apparent drought and some level of ensuing famine. Life was better, but it was not all they had hoped for. This complexity reflects well the human condition. Even when things improve in a fallen world, it is still not *heaven*. Malachi speaks to the entire human experience and tells us that the reality of disappointment with our lives and with God — and thus the biblical invitation to lament — is not relegated to only the most extreme seasons or the most afflicted people. Lament is also for the average God-follower.

6. By this, I mean true in a theological sense. There is at times a distinction between theological truth (what God says is true) and emotional truth (the raw reality of a situation). Lament is a vibrant expression of truth, even when it calls God's character into question. It is true because it is an expression of the angst of the writer's soul. It is honest, thus it is true. Our refusal to give credence and validity to honest emotional expression that conflicts with biblical norms shows how far we have come from biblical spirituality.

7. Brueggemann, 17.

8. Peterson, 119.

CHAPTER 8: WHISPER OF PLEASURE

1. G. K. Chesterton, *Orthodoxy*, rev. ed. (Fort Collins, CO: Ignatius Press, repr. 1995), 70. Chesterton, the rotund and quick-witted literary figure of the early 1900s, articulates a warm, offbeat, and thoroughly intriguing perspective on Christian faith as he recounts his own journey into belief.

2. A certain reading of Pascal, as with many of the medieval writers (particularly the ascetic ones), would suggest a possible conflict between the notion of happiness and pleasure. However, in those face-offs, the notion of pleasure is being used with a narrower intent referring to a debased, neurotic enterprise of selfishly pursuing small, destructive desires. I am using *pleasure* in a broader sense, hoping to redeem its fuller reflection of God's created purpose for his creation.

3. Blaise Pascal, *Pensees, Section VII: Morality and Doctrine*, pense 425, www.classicallibrary.org/pascal/pensees/index.htm.

4. Jonathan Edwards insists that we never forget what God is most passionate about: himself. In his work *The End for Which God Created the World*, Edwards says the movement of all activity is directed toward the ultimate end of echoing glory back to God. This, he reminds us, is no different when God is the one acting. God's ultimate desire is for himself because he is what is ultimately good, ultimately pleasurable, ultimately beautiful. He is what is ultimately worthy of desiring. For any other creature, this would be sadistically neurotic. For God, it is simply truth, what *is*.

5. See Psalm 104:31.

6. Pascal, *Pensees, Section VII: Morality and Doctrine*, pense 425.

7. Chesterton's apologetic style is more an invitation to an adventurous

romance than a set of codes and religious principles. Two chapters in his classic book *Orthodoxy* where I find this bubbling up are "The Paradoxes of Christianity" and "Romance of Orthodoxy."

8. Malachi 3:10.

9. Malachi 4:2.

10. Aquinas's thoughts can be found in his *Summa*, particularly the *Treatise on Habits* questions 74–77 and a long selection of questions dealing with pleasure in his *First Part of the Second Part*. See www.ccel.org/a/aquinas/summa/home.html.

11. This reading takes Paul's words in Romans 7:15 seriously when he evidences his frustration over why he was not doing what he wanted to do (righteousness) and why he kept doing what he did not want to do (sin). From both angles, Paul's desires as a new creation in Christ were good, and his core reality was bent toward God. Obviously, original sin suggests that humanity before a grace encounter with Christ does not experience this new orientation, and further, the struggle against the effects of original sin is not finally conquered until the ultimate end.

12. C. S. Lewis, *Letters to Malcolm: Chiefly on Prayer* (New York: Harcourt, 1992), 89.

13. Lewis, 89.

14. Dallas Willard, *The Divine Conspiracy* (San Francisco: HarperSan-Francisco, 1998), 41.

15. Lewis, 89.

CHAPTER 9: BETWEEN

1. Malachi 4:4.

2. See Malachi 4:5.

3. Interpretations abound as to exactly how this promise of the coming Elijah would be fulfilled. Many Christian scholars hold that it is intricately connected to the coming of Jesus, the Messiah. It appears part of this connection was made through John the Baptist who Luke tells us came "in the spirit and power of Elijah" (Luke 1:17). John the Baptist stepped into history to announce the coming of the Messiah, and the Baptist's ministry was the inauguration of Christ's ministry.

4. This is the title of Robert Benson's 2001 release from HarperCollins, *Between the Dreaming and the Coming True: The Road Home to God.*

5. Some believe that Malachi 4:4-6 is an appendix to the collected prophets rather than just a conclusion to Malachi, enjoining them to the history of Israel and all the other writings as an attempt to connect the Israelites with and remind them of the bigger picture, the broader story of God and his dealings with his people.
6. Certainly many church traditions have a resistance to celebrating much of the Christian calendar, Lent included. This resistance traces it roots back to the Anabaptist reaction against Catholicism and the impression at the time that such celebrations were inventions of Rome. However, with the discovery of several documents from the early church, such as the diaries of Egeria from the fourth century, it seems clear that early Christian practice included the celebration of a number of holy days.
7. Reverend Brook Meyers, Episcopal of the Holy Communion Church, June 21, 2004, www.holycommunion.net.
8. Meyers.
9. Barbara Bradley Hagerty, "Mother Teresa Beatified," *Morning Edition*, NPR, October 14, 2003.
10. I recount this story in *Deeper Walk: God of Mercy, God of Relationship, Vol. 2* (Relevant Books, 2003), exploring more the angle of our sinful need to explain God.
11. Tom Conlon, *Country Dog, City Boy*, private label, 2002.

CHAPTER 10: OF GOD AND FIREFLIES

1. Kathleen Norris, *The Cloister Walk* (New York: Riverhead Books, 1996), 34.
2. Isaiah 24:14-15.
3. This is the paradoxical reason why God's selfishness is not sadistically neurotic, as human selfishness is. God — and only God — is able to give what is truly best to another by rigidly maintaining his own final priority.
4. Perhaps you have picked up that I am something of a skeptic. I'm not proud of this; it just is. I'm growing and repenting, but skepticism dies slowly. I say this because making such a statement ("the Spirit spoke") is itself an act of difficult faith on my part. I know such words come easily for some, and I'm jealous of that. For me, suggesting that God actually *said* something makes me nervous. *Did he really? How can I know? Can I be certain?* So as you see, the underlying questions of this

book are ones I still wrestle with and will, I believe, until heaven. Yet I am learning and being transformed. There is hope.

5. Søren Kierkegaard, *Provocations* (Farmington, PA: The Bruderhof Foundation, 2002), 31.

6. Wendy M. Wright, *Seasons of a Family's Life* (San Francisco: Jossey-Bass, 2003), 35.

7. Romans 8:6, MSG.

author

Winn Collier is a writer, pastor, and spiritual journeyer. The journey is shared with his wife, Miska, and his boys, Wyatt and Seth. You may connect with Winn at www.winncollier.com.